Mediterranean Diet

The Complete Diet Guide for Beginners

Mediterranean Diet Mistakes, Meal Plan & Diet Cookbook

2nd edition

Table of Contents

Introduction 6

Chapter 1: Why Try a Mediterranean Diet? 7

Chapter 2: How and Why This Diet Works................... 10

Chapter 3: Key Ingredients.. 12

Chapter 4: Tips To Make This Lifestyle Work For You....... 17

Chapter 5: Let's Begin with Breakfast......................... 22

Mediterranean Omelet 22

Stick to Your Ribs Breakfast Couscous 23

Pancakes with Honey and Greek Yogurt.................... 24

Potato and Tomato Oven-baked Frittata.................. 25

Peach and Mint Oatmeal....................................... 27

Green Eggs and Toast.. 28

Baked Egg in Portobellos....................................... 29

Broiled Orange or Grapefruit 30

Breakfast Hash with Chicken.................................. 31

Chapter 6: Fresh Salads 32

Bean and Vinaigrette Salad 32

Fresh Kale 33

Barley and Herb Salad 34

Crete Salad with Chicken.. 35

Pasta Salad Mediterranean Style 36

Fresh Mediterranean Salad..................................... 37

Arugula Salad... 38

Roasted Tomato and Eggplant Salad........................ 39

Shrimp and Artichoke Salad 40

Roasted Cauliflower and Couscous Salad 41

Chapter 7: Appetizers Anyone? 43

Lemon-Garlic Marinated Shrimp.............................. 43

Mediterranean Skewer Appetizers and Spicy Vinaigrette Dipping Sauce 44

Tomato Crostini Appetizer 45

Cool Greek Dip... 46

Homemade Hummus 47

Roasted Red Pepper with Feta 48

Salmon Cakes 49

Baked Mussels with Mozzarella 51

Eggplant Mini Pizzas 52

Olive Tapenade 53

Chapter 8: Sandwich Favorites 54

Mediterranean Portobello Burger 54

Grilled Eggplant Parmesan Sandwich 56

Roasted Red Pepper Cheesy Panini 58

Mediterranean for the Halibut Sandwiches 59

Roasted Chicken Pita Pocket 60

Best Bulgur and Chickpea Burger 61

Spinach and Salmon Sandwich with Tzatziki Sauce 63

Delectable White Bean Wrap 65

Enticing Egg Salad Mediterranean Style 66

Grilled Zucchini Wraps 67

Chapter 9: Entrees 68

Salmon Panzanella 68

Simple Mediterranean Shrimp with Pasta 69

Grouper White Fish with Olives 70

White Bean Stew 71

Easy Grilled Salmon 72

Fruit-Glazed Turkey Breast 73

Chicken on the Mediterranean 75

Linguini with Garlic 76

Black Bean and Rice Bake 77

Orange-Mint Lamb Chops 79

Veggie and Halloumi Kebabs 80

Chapter 10: For Your Sweet Tooth 82

Frosty Banana Smoothie with Almond Milk 82

Zesty Poached Pears 83

Orange Ricotta Cake 84

Fruit Salad with Greek Yogurt 85

Rice Pudding 86

Panna Cotta 87

Grilled Peaches with Sweet Cheese Sauce 88

Almond Flour Cookies 90

Halva 91

Pasteli 92

Chapter 11: Snacking Like a Star **93**
Chapter 12: Meal Planning Made Easy **106**
Chapter 13: Mistakes and Misconceptions **112**
Conclusion **119**
Instant Access to Free Book Package! 121

Introduction

Thank you for downloading this book, "Mediterranean Diet: The Complete Diet Guide for Beginners."

When you say the word diet, many people think you mean rice cakes and yogurt in tiny portions. They believe that the only way to diet is to starve. They do not realize that there are delicious and appetizing meals that can be prepared in a way that maintains a healthy lifestyle. Please take the time to read this book and decide for yourself.

The Mediterranean Diet has been acknowledged the world over for adding the fun back into taking care of your health and body. In addition, it is not an overly complicated diet to follow. The parameters of the diet allow a range of meals, from simple to elaborate ones, depending on your preferences. You will see lots of color and flavor in the recipes detailed in this book. The process of 'dieting' can be effective and easy, while also allowing you to take pleasure in food.

Please feel free to share this book with your friends and family. Please also take the time to write a short review on Amazon to share your thoughts.

Chapter 1: Why Try a Mediterranean Diet?

Folks who live in the region that border the Mediterranean Sea have captured the attention of doctors and health researchers for quite some time. It was observed that people living in these areas were living healthier lives than what is observed at many other places in the world. They have some of the longest life expectancies with lesser chronic diseases and health conditions. Their overall health was better with less heart-related problems. The cholesterol levels of the people of this region are on the lower side, and so is the incidence of strokes.

In addition, the cases of Alzheimer's disease, Type II diabetes are also fewer in number. What makes this region relatively free from these diseases that are often associated with lifestyle and old age? After analysis of the factors that generally contribute to these conditions, a few factors are identified. Their daily diets are low in processed foods or fast foods. Their food choices are naturally lower in saturated fats and higher in healthy fats (Omega 3 and 6). There is a focus on preparing meals with fresh foods at home. The objective of these fresh, simple ingredients is not some fancy preparation, but the ease of cooking and good taste.

Why would someone be inclined to consider this diet? Maybe because it is not really a diet in the restrictive sense of the word DIET. In fact, it is adopting a lifestyle that has been simplified over the years using the natural ingredients that are readily available in the Mediterranean region. They focus on preparing meals with gathering the families together to enjoy one another's company and support. Their daily lives are more active than Western cultures. Are you looking to improve your overall health and hopefully cut your risk of developing life-threatening illnesses? Consider altering your current food intake to include some healthy choices from the Mediterranean Sea region. Please consult your personal health care provider before making any changes to your diet. The two of you, together know what is best for your body.

The Mediterranean lifestyle diet can help with having a healthier heart and blood vessels. When these are burdened with higher cholesterol levels, the blood pressure rises causing strain on major parts of the body. The heart can become enlarged when it has to pump harder to keep ample blood supply to the organs. The stress on the vessels leads to plaque accumulation within the veins and cause blockages. The vessels are weakened over time with chronic inflammations increasing our chances of having a stroke. A stroke is a bleed in the brain that causes enough damage to limit body functions, impairing movement of limbs and sometimes loss of speech.

Can this lifestyle improve mood or depression issues? Studies may not show conclusive causal links, but it is well understood that healthier diets will lead to better lifestyles that enhances mood overall and can reduce the chances of depression. Good nutrition and activity will improve our lives.

Choosing less fat-saturated foods and more fruits and vegetables is safe for the whole family, making it easier to continue with the "diet." Look for ways to prepare foods to include the whole family in the preparation stages to spend more quality time with our loved ones. Plus, it can limit your temptations to grab fast food. The Mediterranean way of preparing meals is quick and easy.

Are you looking for a way to stabilize blood sugars? The inclusion of more soluble fiber from legumes and other plant sources into our daily meals has been shown to stabilize blood sugars. This can either help stave off the development of Type II Diabetes or delay some of its devastating effects on our major organs such as liver, kidneys, and skin, to name a few. Recent studies have even pointed to the benefits of fibers in improving cognitive functioning and slowing degradation of mental capacity with aging. More research over time will better define the full spectrum of health benefits, but even the currently acknowledged benefits are enough to warrant serious consideration of this diet.

Would you consider for it weight control? The Mediterranean way focuses on more fruits and vegetables, less saturated fats, more protein, and fiber. All of these factors usually help with weight loss and maintaining a healthier weight over the long run.

Many of the diet regimens are difficult to maintain, simply because they feel restrictive and can become boring over time. You cannot be bored with the Mediterranean Diet. A significant component of the diet is welcoming a lot of fresh ingredients into your kitchen. It means making meals with a spectrum of colors on display. If you find some foods are not to your taste, there are so many alternatives that still fit within the diet regimen that you can explore.

Many people complain that they have to change their whole lifestyle when they are on a diet. They feel they cannot entertain guests, enjoy restaurants or find the diversity of flavors they are seeking. The great thing about the Mediterranean diet is that you will be invited to modify your eating patterns to certain types of foods, but you will not feel like you are limiting yourself. Think natural, but not bland.

Counting calories is a pitfall of most diets. Dieters keep track of the calories religiously for a few days but soon get tired. Before you know it, the plan is out the window, and the snacks are back in the equation. The Mediterranean Diet is based on a comfortable and healthy lifestyle that was enjoyed by most folks in Greece and Southern Italy for centuries before other trends emerged (i.e. more processed foods). This speaks to the sustainability of this diet. Especially in comparison to other more fad-based, white-knuckle diets where people feel like they are holding their breath until they reach their goal, this one has potential to last. You will not be counting calories or weighing your every meal. You will simply be sticking to a very broad group of healthy selections.

If you do not feel like you are denying yourself, it becomes much easier to stick to your plan. You will not be sneaking unhealthy treats in the middle of the night and falling off the wagon. You will feel sated while also knowing that you are moving closer to your health goals.

Chapter 2: How and Why This Diet Works

Most people are drawn to this diet because of the fresh food, not to mention the variety of dishes this cuisine has to offer. Beyond that, people tend to feel better physically and are more energetic after ditching processed foods for the fresher ingredients that forms the backbone of this diet. Indeed, the cultural elements of the Mediterranean lifestyle that are embedded in this diet can really make the difference for those who adopt this lifestyle.

Firstly, the social aspects of this diet opens up new possibilities for many people. The diet is not just about the types of dishes or how you prepare them, but the notion of being social while doing it. The Mediterranean lifestyle is about gathering people around the kitchen and sharing the responsibility of food preparation. In a fast-paced world where we often shove food in our mouths with little time set aside for preparation, this new way of doing things could end up becoming a welcome ritual. Families and friends can return to the age-old notion of breaking bread together and taking the time to enjoy each other's company on a daily basis. The preparation often does not take long, but the time spent in doing so in a social setting would make great memories.

Secondly, the act of preparing fresh foods is a learning process in itself. In a world where the average child's response to the question "where did this food come from?" is "the grocery store", we can see that the indifference towards our food is commonplace. Preparing food at home using fresh ingredients makes it much easier to look at their source. For example, when cutting up a sprig of parsley as opposed to sprinkling it from a dried and pre-chopped jar, the connection to the earth is much more obvious. Further people get to play cooks and chefs at their own homes. They can create masterpieces each night and hone their skills over time. Most people feel a sense of mastery in their kitchen after only a few weeks, getting a good sense of how to cook and become confident to create their own dishes and modify recipes on the fly. Cooking, like any physical activity can be an exercise with a focus on that moment and a feeling of being fully absorbed in the task. This state of mind is described by many as a relaxing and enjoyable state.

Thirdly, eating and living in line with the Mediterranean way of life is less taxing on our bodies. We move away from processed foods that often result in digestive issues.

flatulence, bloating, increased cravings, mood swings, the feeling of being tired or fatigued and even headaches. We move towards foods that are nutrient-rich. It is often easier for our bodies to absorb the vitamins, minerals and macro-nutrients we are seeking. This means freeing up more energy for the body to heal, more energy for our brains to focus on tasks and process thoughts, more energy available for physical activity. This also means less time tending to our ailments and problems, leaving us to live a rich life. Light exercise is part of this lifestyle. Fresh air, good exercise and healthy food, combined together, changes the way we live. We are able to move, stay active, have healthy hearts and avoid strain on our joints by pursuing an active lifestyle with a light approach.

Many diets claim they are promoting a lifestyle and not just a way of eating. However, the Mediterranean Diet actually brings about the change, in its easy-to-love format. The social, inclusive and a better way of living that is promoted and captured in the Mediterranean Diet make the diet highly likeable and increases the adoption.

Chapter 3: Key Ingredients

The daily meals eaten by the people of this area of the world almost always include some of these key ingredients:

- Olive oil is derived from pressing the olive. Extra virgin olive oil is the product of one pressing or a less processed product. It contains monounsaturated fats that are known as a leading contributor to lower blood cholesterol levels. It is considered a good fat by most standards. Without going into the whole chemical make-up, this means it is not a saturated fat. Fats, including good ones, are meant to be consumed moderately and mostly for cooking or dipping purposes. One teaspoon equals one serving. A myth in the world of diets has been the idea that consuming fats will make you fat. Research indicates that fats are an essential component of our diet and they are required for various functions of the body. In fact, Olive oil contains oleic acid which is the main ingredient in "good fat pills" that promote the body's ability to lose weight. This element allows your body to best control cholesterol levels. You can simply consume the olive oil with your food instead of buying pills from a health food store.

- Fresh fruits and vegetables form the foundation of this lifestyle diet. Base every meal around these and fill ¾ of your plate at each meal with them. Your goal is 4-6 servings a day. Servings are considered as 1/2 cup of cooked vegetables and one cup of fresh fruits or vegetables. Keep fresh fruit on hand for fruit salads. These are excellent, easy ways to incorporate more servings in our daily diets. Think nutrient dense dark greens as your core vegetables and bright colors of the fruits. You will be eating tasty food and it will not just be a gustatory treat, but also a treat to your other senses, especially your eyes. A few main vegetables and fruits that you would use in this diet are listed below.

    o Kale

    o Fresh spinach

    o Romaine lettuce

- o Winter squashes

- o Blueberries

- o Cranberries

- o Strawberries

- o Bananas

- o Cherries

- o Melons

- o Tomatoes

- o Peppers

- o Onions

- o Garlic

- o Avocados

- o Figs

- o Grapes

- o Apples

- o Pomegranates

- o Beets

- Fatty fish warrant a special mention. Include fish high in omega-3 fatty acids for a minimum of two times per week. Shellfish such as shrimp and mussels fall into this category as well. Fish that is grilled or baked are best as it maintains all of the good properties without creating negative side effects. No frying. When we fry fish, we can create carcinogens which can lead to the formation of cancer in the body when consumed. Although it's hard to replace the taste of fried food, it will not take long to develop a preference for grilled or baked foods. People often comment that the flavors stand out so much more when the food is not saturated in additional oils, such as when fried. So you get to turn up the taste while turning down the potentially harmful health repercussions. In addition, you also save yourself a lot of additional calories by avoiding frying. One good choice is grouper, a firm, white-fleshed fish that can be baked, broiled, poached, or steamed. It is excellent for a low-fat source of protein full of B vitamins, iron, and potassium. Salmon and tuna steaks are extremely popular choices too for their disease combating, cell strengthening omega-3s. Strive for approximately 4 oz. of these fish per serving. You are probably already starting to notice that fresh, whole foods are at the heart of this diet and indeed, your heart and overall health will thank you.

- Nuts, legumes, unprocessed peanut butter, and almond butter are key choices for plant proteins. These along with the fruits and vegetables make up the bulk of your daily food intake. Popular and good choices are:

  o Almonds

  o Chickpeas (sometimes called garbanzo beans)

  o Walnuts

  o Black beans

  o Olives

  o White beans

  o Sesame seeds

  If you want to expand beyond these common selections, try:

  o Lima beans

  o Pinto beans

  o Red kidney beans

  o Soybeans

  o Fava beans

- Brown, red or yellow lentils

- Black eyes peas

- Wax beans

- Okra

- Green beans

- Whole grains found in lesser processed breads, plus whole grain pastas are used in large part to compliment the fruits and vegetables and add energy-producing carbohydrates. Every meal needs a fruit or vegetable, a protein, a carbohydrate, and a good fat to keep the body fueled each day.

If you are concerned about trading in meat in some meals for the legumes listed above, you can lay your concerns to rest. Protein is an essential part of any diet. Meat can often be an excellent source of protein. That said, pairing a whole grain with a legume will fulfil your protein needs. It means that you can get an equivalent protein source to meats by substituting a combination of beans with whole wheat or whole grain rice for example. In many cases, this alternative can offer an improved source of nutrients over meats because it does not contain saturated fats that are found in many types of meat. So you end up getting lots of good while avoiding the bad. Many people that subscribe to this diet also report that consuming legumes keep them feeling just as full as consuming meat.

- Red wine in moderation. Approximately a 5 oz. serving daily will provide the daily amount, more or less. If you think about the social aspect of this diet, it is easy to see how this lifestyle can suit your needs over the long term. Just picture yourself in your kitchen with your family or friends, enjoying a glass of wine while preparing fresh foods. Now that is an easy sell to most.

- Low-fat dairy products and eggs. Use them sparingly through the week. Use them as accompaniments, not main courses. For instance, if you have a serving of vegetables, you might add some freshly grated cheese to enhance the taste.

  - Up to seven eggs per week, including those cooked in meals

- Mozzarella cheese

- Low fat, Greek-style yogurt

- Skimmed milk

These ingredients are widely available and grocery shopping would suddenly have a new meaning. Once you try the various varieties of each, you would understand what suits your palette better. Many different varieties of a food type taste different. The key thing is to try out things, explore the local produce and experiment.

Chapter 4: Tips To Make This Lifestyle Work For You

Often times when we want to change something, we attempt to change too much too quickly. We are conditioned to expect instant results. This usually causes us to fall short of our goals quickly. The disappointment and frustration can lead us to quit entirely, assuming the plan is just not the right fit for us. Focus on these simple steps or tips to help you follow this diet change. If you are looking to lose weight or feel more energetic, you can do a lot more than just improve your diet. We are not talking about beefing up your body for a competition. What we want to say, is that a little bit of lifestyle change can really enhance the results that are possible out of your diet changes. The integration of exercise and a good diet plan can really give strong results and a lasting impact. It is time to impress yourself with your progress and say goodbye to old habits that leave you with little energy and added pounds.

Focus on these simple steps or tips to help you follow this diet upgrade.

- Active lifestyle. Get moving even if it is parking a few more parking places away from the door. Walk the neighbor's dog if you do not have one yourself. Take a brisk walk a couple of times a week in the beginning and adding one more activity per week until you are walking regularly. Remember activity is cumulative. Four sessions of ten minutes of activity are as good as one long session. Take a moment right now to think of where you could insert this into your daily or weekly routine. Before you jump to what we all initially think -"I'm just too busy, so the diet changes will have to be enough" - just ask yourself where you might start. Is it brisk-walking a lap of the school parking lot while waiting for your kids? Is it getting up from your desk a few times a day to walk a block and clear your head (which could result in improved creativity and ability to focus better according to many studies)? Is there someone else in your life who would want to be your buddy and thus, you could make this a social time as well? Some people even consider organizing walking meetings with colleagues to help integrate healthy habits into the workplace as well. Once you start asking yourself the question of how you could add in activity, you might be surprised by how many ideas you generate. There may be busy days and setbacks here and there. That's normal for any shift or new goal in one's life. However, by creating a habit of moving your body daily, you may find yourself craving this activity and finding more and more opportunities to add it into your everyday routine.

- Family gatherings make mealtimes more meaningful. Start scheduling at least two nights a week to be family nights to prepare the evening meal. The extra time spent with loved ones will lead to the desire to do so more often. This will cut down the number of times your family will eat out as well. That means less spending and less consumption of unhealthy foods. It can also mean an increase in feeling connected to food for everyone. In the long term, research shows this results in better food choices. When people have confidence with cooking and a reasonable knowledge of how to prepare meals, they are more likely to use these skills than rely on "convenience foods" like those which are frozen or pre-cooked. This is a great gift to give to anyone in your life. You can combine being social with being creative and then you all get to enjoy what you have prepared together. Alienation no more.

- Trade out butter or saturated fats and use olive or canola oil instead. This transition can be easy. Simply keep olive oil on your countertop or in a cupboard nearby for ease of use. If your family might resist the slightly different flavor of the oil, be sure to purchase an extra virgin type or one marked "light tasting". The flavor will be palatable and good for your heart. By making a few changes to your fridge and cupboards, you simplify your everyday decision-making. Just make the things available in your house that you want yourself and your family to consume, and the shift to a better lifestyle can be easy. You simply take the time to re-work your kitchen a little so that you are not tempted to consume unhealthy food. Next, you make good decisions at the grocery store. With these two small steps, you take the stress out of making daily decisions about your diet. You can simply go with the flow of how you have already set things up. Out with the butter, in with the extra virgin olive oil. If you happen to consume butter while visiting a friend or out at a restaurant, it is no big deal. However, you can know that you have made good decisions the majority of the time while cooking for yourself.

- Avoid salt by relying on herbs and spices to season foods. Salt has become a common sight on most household and restaurant tables. You probably know that for many people, added salt can cause an increase in blood pressure. If you want to keep it simple, you can find herb blends in most grocery stores that can be sprinkled on nearly anything to enhance the taste. These may contain green herbs, chili, other peppers, even edible flowers. Find the blend that is right for you. You can also create these blends yourself by choosing a few of your favorite flavors and combining them in a jar. If you like adding fresh herbs, then cilantro, basil, and dill can really liven up vegetables and meats.

- Be patient with your transition. Over time, our bodies crave less of the sugar-packed or sodium-filled foods when better alternatives have been used. As we said before, you will not feel the hunger pangs that you may have experienced before with more restrictive diets. You will grow to love the fresh, full taste of things plucked straight from the earth as well as organic meats and fish. You may miss that punch that salt and sugar provide at the beginning. Like any habit we have, our brains and bodies take time to accept something new and release old ways of doing things. With these cravings arise, look at how you can play with elements of the current diet parameters to meet your needs. If you crave something sweet, consider what fruits you may want to buy. If you crave something salty, think of what spices might best meet that craving. Do not let yourself get into a rut of always eating the same thing. If you get bored then you might go back to bad habits. There are a lot of things to try from the Mediterranean Diet so keep it fresh and fun. Try new recipes and rediscover the playfulness that this diet allows.

- Start with small steps: go meatless for one day a week to begin. Choose legumes as the plant protein instead of the meat. Supplement the meal with a side of whole grain pasta. Remember that if the protein is a concern for you, by pairing the legume and the grain together you will make a complete protein that is recognized by your body very similarly to meat alternatives. If you have vegetarian friends, they will likely welcome helping you will this task of learning healthy, simple and delicious recipes. Adding spices and herbs can be a great addition to any vegetarian meal as well.

- Focus on simple cooking procedures. Sauté, broil, grill, steam, or poach as your primary cooking methods. Most of these methods take very little time and save you the mess of frying. They also help keep the nutrients in your food intact. Cooking vegetables along with fish, meat or legumes can make things easy as well. Baking a selection of vegetables along with fish can enrich the flavor of both. Grilling a selection of root vegetables with chicken in the same olive oil and spice mixture can make a great, easy and filling meal. Garlic and onions are your friends too. You can easily liven up any meal by adding either the powdered, dried or the fresh versions of anything in the onion and garlic family and you will look like a chef. The flavors of the meat and veggies will be enhanced, and your company will thank you.

- Limit red meats to a couple of times a month. When you do consume them, be sure to pick lean cuts. A serving size is approximately the size of a deck of cards. Use it as a tasty addition to a salad, not the main course. If you love that feeling of being full after eating meat, consider adding in some legumes for a meal with a reasonable portion of meat. The combination usually works great to make you achieve that satisfaction you are seeking.

- Exchange 2% milk for skim milk. Reach for the low fat cheeses and low fat, higher protein Greek style yogurts. When you add fruit to these, the taste difference is hardly noticeable. If you are using these for savory sauces, once you add in garlic or herbs, you will quickly get used to the lower fat versions. When choosing low-fat alternatives, you can check to make sure that sugar has not been added to mask any difference in taste. Go for the more natural options.

- Try out chilled almond milk. It can add a healthy, nutty taste to your whole grain cereal or snack smoothie. Almonds are an excellent source of fiber and protein, as well as vitamin E and magnesium. Even if no one in your household is lactose intolerant, the good fats as well as the nutrients are good for everyone.

- Prepare meals or snacks in advance for quick access. People start losing the battle with their bad habits when they are unprepared. They find themselves grabbing for convenience foods at the corner store or stopping by the drive-thru on the way to their next errand. Be your own best friend and come prepared, so you do not have to test your willpower. You can resist the temptation of reaching for a highly processed packaged snack, by having a serving of fresh, delicious fruit ready to be consumed. Crunchy fresh vegetables with a side of Greek yogurt dip can be an excellent alternative to greasy potato chips. You can stay on track easily by carrying a snack with you.

Remember to celebrate these small changes as successes. The continued practice will result in the adoption of healthier foods in your life and more importantly, you will appreciate real changes in your body. Avoid the pitfalls of boredom by keeping a variety of foods in your meals. One backslide does not negate the entire process. This is a lifetime of better choices that happen one day at a time, one meal at a time. Focus on the new food introductions so as to not feel deprived. No foods are completely off limits; some are just reserved for very special occasions in moderate servings.

Chapter 5: Let's Begin with Breakfast

Mediterranean Omelet

12 Egg whites (3 per person, making 4 servings)

2 tablespoons of olive oil

3 cups of portobello mushrooms

1 cup of shredded mozzarella cheese

1/2 cup diced onions (red, green or white all work fine)

2 cups fresh spinach (baby or regular, well washed)

Warm a large frying pan over medium-high heat. Add olive oil to warm for a minute, then add the egg whites to the pan. Add the vegetables (the firmer ones like the onions first, followed by the mushrooms, then the spinach.) Fold the omelet over and cook until done. Cover with cheese in the pan until it has melted a little, then serve.

Stick to Your Ribs Breakfast Couscous

3 cups low-fat milk (skim or 1%)

1 small cinnamon stick

1 cup uncooked whole-wheat couscous

1/4 cup dried currants or raisins

1/2 cup chopped dried apricots (into 4 pieces)

6 teaspoons dark brown sugar (divided)

1/4 teaspoon salt

4 teaspoons butter (melted and divided)

In a large saucepan, combine the milk with the cinnamon stick over medium-high heat for 3 minutes or until small bubbles form around the inner edge of the pot, but do not boil. Remove from heat and while still warm, stir in couscous, currants or raisins and apricots. Add 4 teaspoons of the brown sugar, and the salt. Cover the mixture, and let it stand 15 minutes. Remove and discard the cinnamon stick. Divide couscous among 4 bowls, and top each with a teaspoon of melted butter and 1/2 a teaspoon of brown sugar. Serve warm.

Pancakes with Honey and Greek Yogurt

1 cup uncooked, old-fashioned oats

1/2 cup all-purpose flour (or whole wheat flour for a denser pancake)

2 tablespoons of whole flax seeds.

1 teaspoon of baking soda

1/4 teaspoon of salt

2 cups Greek yogurt (plain, vanilla or a flavor of your liking)

2 large eggs

2 tablespoons of honey (plus more to drizzle on top while serving)

2 tablespoons of canola oil

Toppings: fresh fruit or sweeter options like chocolate or syrup

Combine first five ingredients in a blender and pulse for 30 seconds. Then add the yogurt eggs, oil, and honey and blend until smooth. Let batter stand to thicken at room temperature for about 20 minutes.

Heat a large non-stick skillet over medium heat. Brush the skillet with canola oil. Ladle the batter in ½ cup portions onto the skillet. Cook pancakes until bottoms are golden brown and bubbles form on top, then flip until other side is golden brown. Serve immediately or transfer to a baking sheet and keep warm in the oven until ready to serve Serve with desired toppings and honey drizzled over.

Potato and Tomato Oven-baked Frittata

1/2 cups chopped potatoes (roughly 2 medium potatoes)

tablespoons extra virgin olive oil

medium red onion (chopped fine)

0g pancetta (chopped coarsely)

cup baby spinach

cups red grape tomatoes (cut into halves)

red pepper (chop into small pieces)

large eggs

/2 cup thickened cream

/2 cup shredded parmesan cheese (fresh is best)

/4 cup grated cheddar cheese

reheat oven to 200°C while preparing the ingredients.

lace the chopped potatoes in a heatproof, microwave-safe bowl. Microwave on high for
minutes or until tender. Allow to cool.

eanwhile, warm the oil in a non-stick frying pan over medium-high heat. Add the onion
nd stir while cooking for 3-4 minutes. Add the pancetta. Continue to cook while stirring
or 3 to 5 minutes or until onion is tender and pancetta is golden brown. Add in the spinach.
ook for 1 minute or until spinach is just beginning to wilt.

ombine onion-pancetta mixture, tomatoes and red pepper in a large bowl. Lightly grease
large oven ready dish. Arrange half the potato, in a single layer, over the greased dish.
op with half the onion mixture. Repeat with remaining potato and onion mixture.

Whisk eggs and cream in a medium bowl. Carefully pour the egg mixture over vegetable
nixture, then sprinkle with parmesan and grated cheddar cheese. Bake for roughly 30

minutes or until egg mixture is set and beginning to brown on top. Let stand at room temperature for 5 minutes then serve.

Peach and Mint Oatmeal

/2 cup Old fashioned rolled oats

/2 cup skim milk

/2 cup water

tablespoon packed light brown sugar or granulated sugar

/8 teaspoon cinnamon or nutmeg (optional)

dash salt

/4 teaspoon vanilla extract

/2 cup diced fresh peaches (canned can also work if need be and in that case, drain the excess liquid)

tablespoons of cream or half-and-half

tablespoons fresh mint leaves (chopped coarsely)

Honey (to top after cooking if desired)

n a large microwave-safe bowl, combine together oats, milk, water, sugar, optional innamon or nutmeg and salt. If you use fresh peaches, then add them to the oatmeal mixture before microwaving so, they will cook and become soft. Mix well and then microwave on high setting for 3 to 4 minutes. Remove from microwave and stir in the vanilla extract. If using canned peaches fold them into oatmeal after microwaving (as they re already soft). Drizzle oatmeal with cream and honey if desired. Serve warm.

Green Eggs and Toast

2 small ripe avocados (remove pit and remove from skin)

1/3 cup soft feta (crumble)

2 tablespoons chopped fresh cilantro (plus extra to garnish)

Squeeze of fresh lemon or lime juice to taste

4 large eggs

4 large slices rye or whole grain bread

Salt and pepper to taste

Place the avocado in a medium size bowl and mash with a fork. Add the cilantro and squeeze a large lemon or lime juice and mash until combined fully. Season to taste with sea salt and freshly ground black pepper.

Fry the eggs in olive oil to your preference. Over medium can be good on toast as the yolks will be soft but not runny.

Toast or grill with a little butter the rye or whole grain bread until golden brown. To serve spoon 1/4 of the avocado mixture onto each slice of bread, then place the egg on top. Sprinkle the feta and serve immediately garnished with the extra cilantro.

Baked Egg in Portobellos

large portobello mushrooms (remove the stem and wipe clean)

xtra virgin olive oil spray (make your own using a spray bottle or purchase)

/2 teaspoon salt, divided

/2 teaspoon freshly ground black pepper, divided

/2 teaspoon garlic powder

large eggs

tablespoons grated Parmesan or Romano cheese

tablespoons chopped parsley for garnish

reheat your broiler on high. Set your oven rack in the middle of the oven. Line a baking heet with aluminum foil.

pray the mushroom caps with the extra virgin olive oil cooking spray on both sides. prinkle with 1/4 teaspoon salt, a dash of pepper and 1/4 teaspoon garlic powder. Broil or 5 minutes on each side or until just beginning to become tender.

emove mushrooms from oven. Switch oven from broil to bake, setting the temperature o 400 degrees.

reak an egg into each mushroom, leaving the yolk intact. Sprinkle cheese over the egg, hen bake for 15 minutes or until egg whites are cooked fully.

prinkle the eggs with the remaining salt and pepper. Garnish with parsley and serve.

Broiled Orange or Grapefruit

2 large grapefruits (white or red) or 2 large oranges

3 tablespoons of honey

2 teaspoons of powdered ginger

2 teaspoons of cinnamon

1 banana (medium ripe)

1 tablespoon of canola oil

Preheat your broiler to medium heat. Slice the oranges or grapefruits in half as if you were going to eat them as is (not from stem to stem). Drizzle honey over the freshly cut fruit. Toss the ginger powder and the cinnamon on top. Slice the banana thinly and place over the honey and spice (3-5 slices per half grapefruit or half orange).

Place the fruits flat side down (banana side down) onto a sheet greased with a thin coating of canola oil. Pay close attention as they broil making sure not to burn them. Aim to only slightly brown the top.

Relish the fruit with a grapefruit knife and spoon.

Breakfast Hash with Chicken

2 boneless, skinless chicken thighs cut into chunks (roughly 1 1/2 cups)

1 medium sweet potato or approximately 2 cups (peel and dice)

1/2 cup onion (chopped coarsely)

Pinch of salt

Extra virgin olive oil

Parsley, cilantro, chili flakes and/or a fried egg for garnish if desired.

In a large skillet, heat 2 teaspoons of extra virgin olive oil over medium-high heat. Toss the chicken with a pinch of salt then add to the heated pan and cook until chicken is browned and cooked through. Remove the chicken from the pan and set aside. Add 1 tablespoon of extra virgin olive oil to the pan. Then add the sweet potato, onion and a pinch of salt. Cook until sweet potatoes are tender and onions are browned. Add the chicken back to the pan and toss to combine. Add additional herbs or a fried egg to complete and serve.

Chapter 6: Fresh Salads

Bean and Vinaigrette Salad

2 tablespoons balsamic vinegar

1/3 cup fresh parsley, chopped

4 garlic cloves, finely chopped

Ground black pepper, to taste

1/4 cup extra-virgin olive oil

1 can (15 ounces) garbanzos, rinsed and drained

1 can (15 ounces) black beans, rinsed and drained

1 medium red onion, diced

Lettuce leaves

1/2 cup celery, finely chopped

Create the vinaigrette in a bowl, whisk together the parsley, garlic, pepper most importantly, the balsamic vinegar, slowly whisk in the olive oil. Set aside.

In another bowl, put the beans and onion together. Pour the vinaigrette over the mixtur and toss in order to coat evenly. Cover and refrigerate.

To serve, put 1 lettuce leaf on the plate. Divide the salad among the individual plates an garnish with chopped celery. Serve immediately. This will serve six people.

Fresh Kale

12 cups chopped kale

2 tablespoons lemon juice

1 tablespoon olive oil, or as needed

1 tablespoon minced garlic

1 teaspoon of soy sauce

Black pepper to taste fresh ground is better

Steam the kale in a steamer for approximately 7-10 minutes. Whisk together remaining ingredients and toss with the cooked kale.

Barley and Herb Salad

1 cup of barley

2 ½ cups water

6 or 7 sundried tomatoes

2 cloves of garlic

2 tbsp. olive oil plus 2 more

1 tbsp. balsamic vinegar

4 oz. chopped black olives

½ cup chopped basil

Bring barley and water to a boil in a saucepan over high heat. Reduce heat to medium low, cover, and simmer about 30 minutes. Drain and cool to room temperature in a bowl

Puree the sundried tomatoes, garlic, two tablespoons olive oil, and balsamic vinegar in a blender until smooth. Pour over the barley. Fold in the basil, olives, and remaining olive oil until blended. Cover and refrigerate until ready to serve.

Crete Salad with Chicken

1/3 cup red-wine vinegar

2 tablespoons extra-virgin olive oil

1 tablespoon chopped fresh dill or oregano or 2 tablespoons dried

1 teaspoon garlic powder

1/4 teaspoon salt

1/4 teaspoon freshly ground pepper

6 cups chopped romaine lettuce

2 1/2 cups chopped cooked chicken

2 medium tomatoes, chopped

1 medium cucumber, peeled, seeded and chopped

1/2 cup finely chopped red onion

1/2 cup sliced ripe black olives

1/2 cup crumbled feta cheese

Whisk vinegar, oil, dill (or oregano), garlic powder, salt, and pepper in a large bowl. Add lettuce, chicken, tomatoes, cucumber, onion, olives, and feta; toss to coat.

Pasta Salad Mediterranean Style

8 ounces multigrain pasta

Zest and juice of 1 lemon

2 teaspoons olive oil

1 13.5- ounce can artichoke hearts packed in water, drained and chopped

8 ounces fresh part-skim mozzarella cheese, chopped

1/4 cup chopped bottled roasted red bell pepper

1/4 cup chopped fresh parsley

1/2 cup frozen peas

Cook pasta according to package instructions, omitting fat and salt.

While pasta is cooking, combine zest and juice of 1 lemon and 2 teaspoons olive oil in a bowl; stir well with a whisk. Put in cheese, artichoke hearts, bell pepper and parsley. Toss to combine all the ingredients

Put peas in a colander; when the pasta is cooked, drain the pasta over the peas. Shake well to drain all the remaining water, but do not run under cold water. Add the pasta and peas to the artichoke mixture, and toss well until the mixture is combined. Serve warm or at room temperature.

Fresh Mediterranean Salad

1 (8-ounce) English cucumber

2 tablespoons fresh lemon juice

2 tablespoons extra-virgin olive oil

Black pepper, to taste

6 cups watercress or like salad greens

1 can artichoke hearts, drained and quartered

2 large celery stalks, sliced

1/2 cup sliced red onion

1/2 cup feta cheese

Cut cucumber in half, and slice crosswise into 1/4-inch-thick slices. Process 3/4 cup cucumber and lemon juice in a blender. Add olive oil in a thin stream; pulse until combined. Season the dressing with black pepper, to taste; transfer to a large bowl. Add remaining 1 cup cucumber, salad, artichoke hearts, celery, red onion, and feta cheese to a bowl. Toss with the dressing before serving.

Arugula Salad

4 cups chopped Arugula greens

Cup chopped grape tomatoes

¼ nuts of choice

2 tbsp. olive oil

1 tbsp. balsamic vinegar

1 sliced avocado

¼ grated parmesan cheese

Ground pepper to taste

Blend dressing ingredients with the cheese. Then toss with greens, tomatoes, and avocado. Dust with grated cheese.

Roasted Tomato and Eggplant Salad

This is a great option for a meal because it can be served warm or cold.

2 medium eggplants (roughly 3 cups cubed)

6 or 7 medium-sized tomatoes (roughly 3 cups cubed)

5-6 tablespoons olive oil (ideally extra virgin)

1/4 teaspoon salt

3 tablespoons red wine vinegar or balsamic if you prefer

1/4 cup pine nuts

1/4 cup parmesan cheese (finely grated)

4-5 large basil leaves (diced finely)

Preheat oven to 450 degrees while preparing your vegetables. Take two baking sheets and line with aluminum foil.

Toss eggplant with 2 tablespoons of olive oil and a dash of salt, then place on one baking sheet (spread out evenly). Cut the tomatoes into 1" cubes and toss with 2 tablespoons of olive oil and a dash of salt. Place on second baking sheet.

Place both baking sheets in oven for 30 minutes or until eggplant is soft and begins to darken at the edges. Remove both baking sheets from oven and let cool for at least 10 minutes.

Place eggplant and tomato, vinegar, remaining olive oil and pine nuts together in a large bowl and toss. Top with basil and parmesan cheese. You can serve while still semi-warm or you can cover and let marinate in the basil and vinegar overnight for a more intense flavor.

Shrimp and Artichoke Salad

2 tablespoons extra virgin olive oil

1 teaspoon lemon juice (or lime juice alternatively if desired)

1/2 pound medium cooked shrimp (peeled and deveined)

1 (14-ounce) can artichoke hearts, drained and coarsely chopped (roughly into quarters)

2 tablespoons minced red onion (or chives if preferred)

2 tablespoons finely chopped fresh parsley

1/4 teaspoon freshly ground black pepper

Combine olive oil and lemon juice in a medium bowl and stir together. Add shrimp and artichokes to ensure the juice and oil have coated all evenly. Add remaining ingredients and toss gently together. Cover and chill at least 30 minutes to allow flavors to absorb. A dash of salt can be added to enhance the taste if you choose.

Roasted Cauliflower and Couscous Salad

 large head of cauliflower (cut into florets)

 1/2 cups of cherry tomatoes (sliced in half)

/2 red onion (diced)

/3 cup of kalamata olives (finely chop)

 English cucumber (finely chop)

 cup of parsley (finely chop)

/3 cup of pine nuts (leave as is)

/4 teaspoon of red pepper flakes (crush)

 tablespoons of olive oil

 cups of dry couscous (your desired size: fine or coarse)

Dressing:

 tablespoons lemon juice (ideally freshly squeezed)

/2 teaspoon Dijon mustard

 clove of garlic (minced)

/2 teaspoon salt

/4 cup olive oil (extra virgin olive oil preferred for smooth taste)

Salt and pepper to taste if desired

Preheat the oven to 350°F. In a medium bowl, combine the cauliflower florets with the
pine nuts, red pepper flakes and 2 tablespoons of olive oil. Lay them on a parchment-lined
baking sheet (single layer for even cooking) and bake in the oven until slightly browned

(approximately 25 to 35 minutes). At 10 minutes, remove from oven and toss, then replace for remaining time. After fully baked, let sit on the counter to cool for 10 minutes.

Combine together the vegetables (all but the cauliflower) in a large bowl after chopping and dicing. Add 2 tablespoons of olive oil and the chopped parsley. Let sit together while the cauliflower is baking.

Follow instructions on the couscous package for best results. Different sized couscous will work fine for this recipe, but each requires a slightly different equation of water to couscous and a different time to let sit. Typically, fine couscous uses a 1:1 ratio, which means 2 cups of couscous can be combined in a medium bowl with 2 cups of boiling water. Stir together, then cover and let sit for 5 minutes. The water should be fully absorbed, and the couscous should be at the desired softness. If it needs more time, you can stir gently, cover and let sit another 5 minutes. When the water is fully absorbed, stir gently and let sit uncovered for 10 minutes.

For the salad dressing, combine the dijon mustard, lemon juice, garlic and salt in a small bowl. Whisk together and drizzle with olive oil for best consistency.

Once the warm ingredients have cooled for 10 minutes, add the cauliflower and couscous together (gently folding together). Add the remaining cold vegetable mixture and toss together with care. You can serve immediately or cover and let sit until meal time.

Chapter 7: Appetizers Anyone?

Lemon-Garlic Marinated Shrimp

3 tablespoons minced garlic

2 tablespoons extra-virgin olive oil

1/4 cup lemon juice

1/4 cup minced fresh parsley

1/2 teaspoon kosher salt

1/2 teaspoon pepper

1 1/4 pounds cooked shrimp

Place garlic and oil in a skillet and cook over medium heat until fragrant (about 1 minute.) Add lemon juice, parsley, salt, and pepper. Toss them with shrimp in a bowl to combine. Chill until ready to serve.

Mediterranean Skewer Appetizers and Spicy Vinaigrette Dipping Sauce

1/2 cup tomato juice

1/8 teaspoon Worcestershire sauce

2 celery hearts, finely diced (about 3 tablespoons)

1/4 teaspoon kosher salt

1/4 teaspoon freshly ground black pepper

Bocconcini (small mozzarella cheese bites)

Grape tomatoes, artichoke hearts, and Kalamata olives

1/8 teaspoon hot sauce

1/4 teaspoon prepared horseradish

2 tablespoons extra-virgin olive oil

In a medium bowl, whisk together tomato juice, Worcestershire, hot sauce, horseradish, oil, celery, salt, and pepper. Refrigerate until ready to serve as the dipping sauce.

Onto each skewer, thread a Bocconcini ball, tomato, artichoke, and olive; serve with vinaigrette dipping sauce.

Tomato Crostini Appetizer

4 plum tomatoes, chopped

1/4 cup minced fresh basil

2 teaspoons olive oil

1 clove garlic, minced

Freshly ground pepper

Crusty Italian bread cut into 4 slices and toasted

Combine tomatoes, basil, oil, garlic and pepper in a medium bowl. Cover and let stand 30 minutes. Divide tomato mixture with any juices among the toast. Serve at room temperature.

Cool Greek Dip

1 cup Greek low-fat yogurt

1 diced cucumber

1 minced garlic clove

2 tsp. of lemon juice

Ground black pepper

Chopped fresh dill about 3 tbsp.

2 tbsp. olive oil

Blend all ingredients and chill in the refrigerator for 8 hours before serving. This dip works well with fresh vegetables as well as breads and crackers. Further, you can use this as a sauce to add to a sandwich or to accompany a main meat, fish or seafood dish.

Homemade Hummus

2 cloves of garlic one chopped

A can of drained garbanzo beans. Retain half the water.

4 tbsp. of lemon juice

2 tbsp. extra virgin olive oil

2 tbsp. tahini (ground sesame seeds)

In a blender, chop the garlic. Pour garbanzo beans into a blender, reserving about a tablespoon for garnish. Place lemon juice, tahini, chopped garlic and salt in the blender. Blend until creamy and well-mixed.

Transfer the mixture to a medium serving bowl. Sprinkle with pepper and pour olive oil over the top. Garnish with reserved garbanzo beans.

Roasted Red Pepper with Feta

1/4 cup fat-free feta cheese

2 tablespoons fat-free blue cheese dressing

2 whole roasted red peppers, divided in half, with each half cut into strips

4 teaspoons olive oil

Freshly ground black pepper, to taste

2 tablespoons chopped fresh basil plus 4 small leaves for garnish

In a small bowl, combine the feta cheese and the blue cheese dressing. Stir to mix evenly.

Arrange the equivalent of 1/2 red pepper on a plate. Drizzle each serving with 1 teaspoon olive oil and 1 tablespoon of the feta-blue cheese mixture. Sprinkle black pepper and 1/2 tablespoon chopped basil over the salad. Garnish each with a basil leaf and serve at room temperature. Serves four.

Salmon Cakes

/2 pound or 250 g fresh local salmon (where available)

/4 cup small-diced chives (or red onion alternatively)

large stalks of celery (finely diced)

small-diced yellow <u>and</u> red bell pepper (roughly 1/2 cup each)

/4 cup fresh parsley (minced)

tablespoon capers (drain)

/4 teaspoon hot sauce or ½ teaspoon chili flakes alternatively

slices stale bread (remove crusts) for bread crumbs

tablespoons extra virgin olive oil, divided

teaspoons Dijon mustard

extra-large eggs (beat lightly)

alt and freshly ground black pepper to taste

ave extra virgin olive oil on hand for frying

tart by adding a light coating of extra virgin olive oil along with a dash of salt and pepper to the salmon and placing it on a baking sheet (skin side down). Bake for 18 to 20 minutes t 350 degrees. Remove from the oven and cover tightly with aluminum foil. Allow to sit nd cool at room temperature for 10-15 minutes and then place in the refrigerator until old.

n a large grilling pan, add together the 2 tablespoons of olive oil, the chives, diced celery, oth the bell peppers, the minced parsley, capers, hot sauce (or chili flakes), 1/2 teaspoon alt, and 1/2 teaspoon pepper. Over medium heat, toss together gently until the egetables are soft (but not overcooked) which may take approximately 15 minutes. emove from heat and let cool to room temperature.

Break the stale bread slices into pieces and place in a food processor until made in crumbs (this makes approximately 1 cup of bread crumbs). Remove from food process and place onto a dry baking sheet and toast in the oven for 5 minutes Remove after th become slightly browned. Toss occasionally so they do not burn.

Take the chilled salmon and break into small pieces into a large bowl. Add in the toast bread crumbs, mustard, and eggs. Then add in the vegetable mixture and mix togeth well. Cover with lid, foil or plastic and let stand in the refrigerator for 25 minutes. On chilled, the mixture should be a little firmer and easier to shape into patties. The mixtu should make 10 cakes of roughly 1/3 cup each in size.

Next, take a large frying pan over medium heat and warm 2 tablespoons of extra virg olive oil. Fry the patties in batches that allow for enough room to fry evenly for 3 to minutes on each side, until both sides turn golden. Let sit on paper towels once fried absorb excess oil. Serve warm either directly after frying or keep warm in the oven at 2! degrees until meal time.

Baked Mussels with Mozzarella

1 pound of fresh mussels

1/2 cup freshly grated mozzarella cheese

1/4 bread crumbs

2 large eggs

2 tablespoons of extra virgin olive oil

4 cloves of garlic (finely chop)

1 tablespoon of fresh parsley (finely chop)

Freshly ground black pepper to taste

Preheat oven to 400 degrees. Rinse the mussels under fresh water. With a knife, carefully open each mussel. Remove half of the shell and leave the meat on the other half to be dressed and baked.

In a medium bowl, mix all ingredients together to form the batter. Place the mussels on a baking sheet and add batter until the mussels are all completely covered (This will avoid drying out during baking).

Bake for 15-20 minutes on the top shelf of the oven or until the batter turns golden brown and begins to become crispy. Serve hot.

Eggplant Mini Pizzas

2 large eggplants (cut into slices 1 inch thick)

24 oz jar tomato sauce

20 slices provolone cheese (round slices roughly the circumference of the eggplant slice)

1 cup fresh cherry tomatoes (sliced into 3-4 pieces each)

1 cup fresh spinach

1/2 teaspoon salt

Chili flakes or freshly ground black pepper as desired

Preheat the oven to 425 degrees. Using two baking trays, arrange the sliced eggplant (not overlapping). Sprinkle the salt over the slices and bake for 15-20 minutes to start to soften the eggplant.

Remove the eggplant from the oven and turn on your broiler. Keeping the eggplant as is, spread 1 tablespoon of tomato sauce over each slice followed by one slice of provolone cheese. Top with fresh spinach and cherry tomatoes as if you were dressing a pizza. Broil for 3-5 minutes, while watching to ensure it does not burn. The broiler is unforgiving so make sure to keep a close watch.

Serve hot. To make this into a meal, you can also serve as a sandwich by adding fresh bread and sauce of your choosing.

Olive Tapenade

200g whole black olives (kalamata work best)

3 tablespoons of capers (be sure to rinse well as to minimize the salty taste)

2 anchovies if desired (well rinsed and roughly chopped)

1 large clove of garlic (crushed)

2 teaspoon fresh thyme (finely chopped)

Juice of half a medium-sized lemon

5 tablespoons of extra virgin olive oil

With a flavor as strong as olives, a small bowl is often enough to compliment any pre-meal appetizer spread. A teaspoon on a piece of baguette is packed with flavor and will suffice.

If you purchased olives with pits still in, use a pitter or knife to remove all of the pits. Place in a food processor with the rinsed capers, anchovies, garlic, and thyme. Process until pureed and smooth. Squeeze in the lemon juice and while still spinning, add in the olive oil. Additional pepper, salt or lemon juice can be added if desired.

Chapter 8: Sandwich Favorites

Mediterranean Portobello Burger

A 30 minute to make meal high in good fat, lower calorie and high in protein

1 clove garlic, minced

1/2 teaspoon kosher salt

2 tablespoons extra-virgin olive oil, divided

4 Portobello mushroom caps, stems, and gills removed

4 large slices country-style sourdough bread, cut in half

1/2 cup sliced jarred roasted red peppers

1/2 cup chopped tomato

1/4 cup crumbled reduced-fat feta cheese

2 tablespoons chopped pitted Kalamata olives

1 tablespoon red-wine vinegar

1/2 teaspoon dried oregano

2 cups loosely packed mixed baby salad greens

Preheat the grill to medium-high.

Mash the garlic and salt on a cutting board until it's a smooth paste. Mix the paste with 1 tablespoon of oil in a dish. Lightly brush the oil mixture over portabellas and then on one side of the slices of bread

Put the red peppers, tomato, feta, olives, vinegar, oregano and the remaining 1 tablespoon oil in a medium bowl.

Grill the mushroom until tender. It'll take about 4 minutes per side; grill the bread until crispy, taking about 1 minute per side.

Toss salad greens with the red pepper mixture. Place the grilled mushrooms topside down on the half-slices of the bread. Fill the burger with salad mixture and the remaining bread.

Grilled Eggplant Parmesan Sandwich

1 eggplant, (1 1/4-1 1/2 pounds), cut into 12 1/4-inch-thick rounds

Canola or olive oil cooking spray

1/4 teaspoon salt

3 tablespoons finely shredded Parmesan or Asiago cheese

1/2 cup shredded part-skim mozzarella cheese

4 small pieces focaccia bread, or rustic Italian bread

2 teaspoons extra-virgin olive oil

5 ounces baby spinach

1 cup crushed tomatoes, preferably fire-roasted

3 tablespoons chopped fresh basil, divided

Preheat the grill to medium-high.

Put the eggplant rounds on a baking sheet and sprinkle with salt. Coat both sides lightly with cooking spray. Combine the cheeses: Parmesan (or Asiago) and mozzarella in a bowl. Brush both sides of focaccia (or bread) with oil.

Place the spinach in a microwave-safe bowl. Cover it with plastic wrap and punch several holes in the wrap. Microwave on High until wilted, 2 to 3 minutes. Combine tomatoes and 2 tablespoons basil in another microwave-safe bowl. Cover and microwave until bubbling, about 2 minutes.

Place all your ingredients on the baking sheet with the eggplant and take it to the grill. Grill the eggplant slices until brown and soft on both sides, about 2 to 3 minutes per side. Grill the bread until toasted, about 1 minute per side. Return the eggplant and bread to the baking sheet. Reduce grill heat from high to medium.

Place 1 eggplant round on top of each slice of bread. Layer as such: 1 tablespoon tomatoes, 1 tablespoon wilted spinach, and 1 tablespoon cheese on each slice of eggplant. Repeat with the remaining eggplant, sauce, spinach, and cheese. Sprinkle each stack with some of the remaining basil. Place the baking sheet on the grill, close the lid and grill until the eggplant stack is hot and the cheese is melted, about 5 to 7 minutes.

Roasted Red Pepper Cheesy Panini

1/2 cup Mayonnaise with olive oil, divided

1/4 cup chopped fresh basil leaves

2 tablespoons finely chopped oil-cured black olives

8 slices rustic whole grain bread (about 1/2-inch thick)

1 small zucchini, thinly sliced

4 slices provolone cheese

1 jar (7 oz.) roasted red peppers, drained and sliced

Combine 1/4 cup mayonnaise with olive oil, basil with olives in small bowl. Evenly spread bread slices with mayonnaise mixture, then layer 4 bread slices with zucchini, provolone and peppers. Top with remaining 4 bread slices.

Spread remaining mayonnaise on outside of sandwiches and cook in 12-inch non-stick skillet or grill pan over medium heat, turning once, until sandwiches are golden brown and cheese is melted (about 4 minutes).

Mediterranean for the Halibut Sandwiches

 (6-ounce) halibut fillets, skinned

osher salt and freshly ground black pepper

 tablespoons plus 1 tsp olive oil, divided

 (14-ounce) loaf ciabatta bread, ends trimmed, split in half horizontally

 garlic clove, halved

/4 cup reduced-fat mayonnaise

/4 cup chopped sun-dried tomatoes

/4 cup chopped fresh basil

 tablespoons chopped fresh flat-leaf parsley

 tablespoon capers, drained and mashed

rated zest of 1 large lemon

 packed cups (2 ounces) arugula

reheat oven to 450°.

pray a small baking dish with cooking spray; add halibut and season with a pinch each alt and pepper; rub with 1 teaspoon oil. Bake 10-15 minutes, until cooked through and he flesh flakes easily with a fork. Cool.

emove some bread from the top half of loaf. Brush cut sides with 2 tablespoons olive oil. ake on a baking sheet 6-8 minutes, until golden. Rub toasted surfaces with garlic.

n a medium bowl, combine mayonnaise, sun-dried tomatoes, basil, parsley, capers, and emon zest. Add fish, flaking and mixing with a fork. Spoon onto bottom half of bread and op with arugula. Add top of bread and cut into 4 sandwiches.

Roasted Chicken Pita Pocket

1/2 cup (2 ounces) crumbled feta cheese

1/2 cup plain Greek-style yogurt

1 tablespoon chopped fresh dill

1 tablespoon extra-virgin olive oil, divided

1 1/4 teaspoons bottled minced garlic, divided

1/2 teaspoon dried oregano

2 cups sliced roasted store bought rotisserie chicken

4 pitas, cut in half

1 cup chopped lettuce

1/2 cup chopped peeled cucumber

1/2 cup chopped tomato

1/4 cup thinly sliced red onion

Combine feta cheese, yogurt, dill, 1 teaspoon oil, and 1/4 teaspoon garlic in a small bowl, stirring well.

Heat remaining 2 teaspoons olive oil in a large skillet over medium-high heat. Add remaining 1 teaspoon garlic and oregano to the pan, and sauté for 20 seconds. Add chicken, and cook for 2 minutes or until thoroughly heated. Place 1/4 cup chicken mixture in each pita half, and top with 2 tablespoons yogurt mixture, 2 tablespoons shredded lettuce, 1 tablespoon cucumber, and 1 tablespoon tomato.

Best Bulgur and Chickpea Burger

1/2 cup chopped red onion (alternatively chives or white onion will suffice)

1 tablespoon extra virgin olive oil (have extra on hand for grilling)

1/2 cup bulgur

1 cup water

1 cup canned chickpeas (rinsed and drained)

1/4 cup walnuts or cashews

2 garlic cloves (chopped coarsely)

1/2 cup fresh cilantro (chopped coarsely)

1/4 teaspoon ground cumin

1/4 teaspoon cayenne pepper

Have salt and freshly ground black pepper on hand

1/4 teaspoon finely grated lime or lemon zest

1/2 teaspoon fresh lime or lemon juice

4 slices multi-grain or whole grain toast

You can add cheese, lettuce and/or sliced tomato to complete the burger.

Warm up a small saucepan and add a tablespoon of olive oil and a dash of salt to half of the portion of chopped red onion. Stir until onion has browned. Add the bulgur and water and cook over low heat until water is absorbed (coward) which may take 15 to 20 minutes. Transfer to a bowl and add the chickpeas.

Pulse bulgur mixture in a food processor with the walnuts (or cashews), garlic, cilantro, cumin, cayenne pepper, 1/4 teaspoon salt, 1/2 teaspoon pepper, lime (or lemon) zest and remaining fresh chopped onion in a food processor until finely chopped.

Take the mixture and separate into 4 even parts, making 4 burgers. Round into patties then let it chill in the refrigerator to help harden for at least 10 minutes before frying.

Add 2 tablespoons of olive oil to a medium-sized pan and warm. Add in the four burgers so they can cook without touching (cooking evenly). Cook for 3-5 minutes over medium heat on each side or until brown and firm.

Serve the burgers open-faced on the multi-grain toast with lime juice drizzled over.

Spinach and Salmon Sandwich with Tzatziki Sauce

4 portions of fresh salmon (often 2 filets cut into 2 portions each will work well)

4 whole grain buns or 4 slices whole grain baguette

4 slices of mozzarella or goat cheese

4 slices of tomato

4 slices of lettuce or spinach (or other leafy green)

Sauce:

2 1/2 cups Greek yogurt (Balkan style yogurt is best for making the sauce thick)

1 large cucumber

1 large clove of garlic (mince or press)

1 tablespoon fresh mint (chopped coarsely)

1 1/2 tablespoons white wine vinegar

2 tablespoons extra virgin olive oil

1/2 teaspoon table salt (or more as needed for desired taste)

To prepare the sauce, start by peeling and removing any seeds from the cucumber. Grate the cucumber and place in a colander. Sprinkle salt over and let drain off any water for 10 minutes. The more water released, the thicker the sauce will be in the end. After 10 minutes, use a potato masher to press any additional water out of the cucumber.

Move cucumber to a bowl and add in the minced garlic and the chopped mint. Add in the other ingredients (vinegar and olive oil) then the yogurt last. Mix together gently, cover and let sit in the refrigerator for an hour.

Grill the salmon in a frying pan over medium heat with a little olive oil (flipping only once) for 2-5 minutes on each side. Dress the bun or baguette with cheese and veggies then place the burger and top with tzatziki sauce to your liking.

Delectable White Bean Wrap

cans or roughly 3 cups cooked white beans

bunch curly leaf parsley

pound of grape or cherry tomatoes

large cloves of garlic

tablespoons of extra virgin olive oil

tablespoons of freshly squeezed lemon juice

/2 tablespoon fresh ground pepper

/4 teaspoon salt

/2 cup feta cheese

large pita (6 x 1/2 pita each, serving 6 people or 4 heaping portions for a hungrier udience)

eafy greens and sliced tomatoes if desired

Drain and rinse the white beans. Rinse the parsley and finely chop. Rinse the tomatoes nd slice them in halves. Combine the beans, parsley, and tomato in a bowl. Add the minced garlic followed by the olive oil, lemon juice, salt, and pepper. Stir in the crumbled eta.

Slice the pita breads in half and open up gently in order to stuff. Adding in slices of leafy greens or tomatoes is recommended before adding the bean mixture. Add in the bean mixture and top with more feta if desired, as well as salt and pepper.

The white bean mixture can be made the night before and prepared into sandwiches just before consuming.

Enticing Egg Salad Mediterranean Style

8 large hard boiled eggs

1/2 cup sun-dried tomatoes (drain off oil and chop into small pieces)

1/2 cup green or red onion (finely chop)

1/2 cucumber (chopped into small pieces)

1/4 cup kalamata olives (diced)

1/2 cup plain Greek yogurt (Balkan style is best as it is thicker)

Juice from half of a lemon

1 1/2 teaspoons of oregano

1/4 teaspoon cumin

1/2 teaspoon sea salt

Freshly ground black pepper on hand as desired

Whole grain bread, wraps or pitas (makes 6-8 portions)

Leafy greens for texture in the sandwich

Let hard-boiled eggs cool to room temperature then chop. Add the eggs to a bowl and then add in sun-dried tomatoes, green or red onions, cucumbers, and olives. Stir in the Greek yogurt, lemon juice, and spices.

Add this to your desired bread with the additional of leafy greens (helps to keep the bread from getting soggy). You prepare this on a Sunday evening and refrigerate, Enjoy it week.

Grilled Zucchini Wraps

4 small zucchinis (cut lengthwise into slices about 1/4 inch)

1 tablespoon extra virgin olive oil

1/8 teaspoon salt (plus more on hand to enhance taste as desired)

1/16 teaspoon of freshly ground black pepper (plus more on hand to enhance taste as desired)

1 1/2 ounces fresh goat cheese

1 tablespoon fresh parsley (chopped coarsely)

1/3 cup fresh basil leaves (Stems removed)

1/2 teaspoon fresh lemon juice

2 cups of fresh, raw baby spinach

4 Wraps (whole wheat or your desired flavor such as sundried tomato)

Warm a pan over medium heat. Add zucchini slices (avoid overlapping) lightly coated in olive oil. Grill until tender then add a dash of salt and pepper to each side.

In a medium bowl, mash together the goat cheese, parsley, and lemon juice using a fork. Generously spread the cheese mixture on the middle third of the wrap. Add the grilled zucchini on top. Lay 3-5 basil leaves along the length of the zucchini and roll up the wrap. You may add additional salt and pepper if needed. Additional fresh veggies such as tomatoes, greens or peppers can be added for additional texture.

Chapter 9: Entrees

Salmon Panzanella

8 Kalamata olives (pit and chop)

3 tablespoons red-wine vinegar

1 tablespoon capers, rinsed and chopped

1/4 teaspoon freshly ground pepper, divided

3 tablespoons extra-virgin olive oil

2 thick slices day-old whole-grain bread, cut into 1-inch cubes

2 large tomatoes, cut into 1-inch pieces

1 medium cucumber, peeled (if desired), seeded and cut into 1-inch pieces

1/4 cup thinly sliced red onion

1/4 cup thinly sliced fresh basil

1 pound center-cut salmon, skinned and cut into 4 portions

1/2 teaspoon kosher salt

Preheat grill to high.

Whisk olives, vinegar, capers and 1/8 teaspoon pepper in a large bowl. Slowly whisk in oil until combined. Add bread, tomatoes, cucumber, onion, and basil.

Oil the grill rack. Season both sides of salmon with salt and the remaining 1/8 teaspoon pepper. Grill the salmon until cooked through, 4 to 5 minutes per side.

Divide the salad among 4 plates and top each with a piece of salmon.

Simple Mediterranean Shrimp with Pasta

2 teaspoons olive oil

2 garlic cloves, minced

1 pound medium shrimp, peeled and deveined

2 cups chopped plum tomato

1/4 cup thinly sliced fresh basil

1/3 cup chopped pitted Kalamata olives

1/4 teaspoon freshly ground black pepper

4 cups hot cooked angel hair whole wheat pasta

1/4 cup (2 ounces) crumbled feta cheese

Heat olive oil in a large non-stick skillet coated with cooking spray over medium-high heat. Add garlic; sauté 30 seconds. Add shrimp; sauté 1 minute. Add tomato and basil; reduce heat, and simmer 3 minutes or until tomato is tender. Stir in Kalamata olives and black pepper. Add cooked shrimp mixture to pasta in a large bowl; toss well. Top with crumbled feta cheese.

Grouper White Fish with Olives

4 grouper fillets or steaks, each 5 ounces and about 1-inch thick

1/2 teaspoon salt

1/4 teaspoon freshly ground black pepper

1 1/2 tablespoons extra-virgin olive oil

1 yellow onion, finely chopped

2 cloves garlic, minced

3 tomatoes, peeled and seeded, then diced

5 large pimiento-stuffed green olives, sliced

1 tablespoon capers, rinsed

1 jalapeno chili, seeded and cut into 1-inch julienne

2 tablespoons fresh lime juice

Sprinkle the grouper steaks on both sides with 1/4 teaspoon of the salt and 1/8 teaspoon of the pepper. In a large, non-stick frying pan, heat 1 1/2 teaspoons of the olive oil over medium-high heat. Add the fish to the pan and sear on both sides until lightly browned about 2 minutes a side. Take fish out and keep warm.

Reduce the heat to medium and add the remaining 1 tablespoon olive oil to the pan. Add the onion and sauté about 6 minutes. Add the garlic and sauté until softened, about 1 minute. Add the tomatoes, olives, capers and jalapeno and simmer for 10 minutes to allow the flavors to blend. Stir in the remaining 1/4 teaspoon salt and 1/8 teaspoon pepper. Return the fish to the pan, cover and simmer until the fish is opaque throughout about 6 to 8 minutes.

Transfer the grouper steaks to warmed individual plates. Stir the lime juice into the vegetables and pan juices and spoon some sauce over each steak. Serve immediately.

White Bean Stew

cups dried cannellini or other white beans, picked over and rinsed, soaked overnight, and drained

cups water

teaspoon salt

bay leaf

tablespoons olive oil

yellow onion, coarsely chopped

carrots, peeled and coarsely chopped

cloves garlic, chopped

/4 teaspoon freshly ground black pepper

tablespoon chopped fresh rosemary

1/2 cups vegetable stock or broth

n a soup pot over high heat, combine the white beans, water, 1/2 teaspoon of the salt, nd the bay leaf. Bring to a boil over high heat. Reduce the heat to low, cover partially, nd simmer until the beans are tender, 60 to 75 minutes. Drain the beans, reserving 1/2 up of the cooking liquid. Remove the bay leaf. Place the cooked beans into a large bowl nd save the cooking pot for later use.

n a small bowl, combine the reserved cooking liquid and 1/2 cup of the cooked beans. Mash with a fork to form a paste. Stir the bean paste into the cooked beans.

Return the cooking pot to the stove top and add the olive oil. Heat over medium-high eat. Stir in the onion and carrots and sauté about 6 to 7 minutes. Stir in the garlic and ook until softened, about 1 minute. Stir in the remaining 1/2 teaspoon salt, the pepper, hopped rosemary, bean mixture, and stock. Bring to a boil, reduce the heat to low and immer until the stew is heated through (about 5 minutes). Serves six.

Easy Grilled Salmon

4 tablespoons chopped fresh basil

1 tablespoon chopped fresh parsley

1 tablespoon minced garlic

2 tablespoons lemon juice

4 salmon fillets, each 5 ounces

Cracked black pepper, to taste

4 green olives, chopped

4 thin slices lemon

This recipe calls for a hot fire in a charcoal grill or heat using a gas grill or broiler. Position the cooking rack that has been sprayed with non-stick spray 4 to 6 inches from the heat source. In a small bowl, combine the basil, parsley, minced garlic, and lemon juice. Spray the fish with cooking spray. Sprinkle with black pepper. Top each fillet the basil-garlic mixture. Place the fish herb-side down on the grill. Grill over high heat. When the edges turn white, after about 3 to 4 minutes, turn the fish over and place on aluminum foil. Move the fish to a cooler part of the grill or reduce the heat. Grill until the fish is opaque throughout or test temperature at the thickest part of the fish for 145 F (about 4 minutes longer). Garnish with green olives and lemon slices when served. Serves four.

Fruit-Glazed Turkey Breast

1-5 pound whole, bone-in turkey breast (thawed)

2 tablespoons chopped fresh rosemary

2 tablespoons fresh thyme leaves, chopped

2 tablespoons olive oil

1 small onion, thinly sliced

1 apple, peeled and thinly sliced

1 pear, peeled and thinly sliced

2 cups apple juice (divided)

1 tablespoon brown sugar

1 tablespoon brown mustard

1 tablespoon olive oil

Preheat the oven to 325 F. Place the turkey breast, skin-side up, on a rack in a roasting pan.

In a small bowl, combine the herbs and the olive oil to make a paste. Smear half of the paste directly on the meat under the skin. Spread the rest of the paste over the top of the skin. In another small bowl, mix together the sliced onions and fruit. Stuff each pocket under the skin with the mixture.

Pour 1 cup of apple juice into the bottom of the roasting pan. Roast the turkey breast for 1 3/4 to 2 hours, until the thickest part of the meat reads 165 F on a meat thermometer. Cover the breast loosely with aluminum foil if the skin starts to get too browned before cooking temperature is reached.

Combine the remaining cup of apple juice, brown sugar, mustard, and olive oil in a saucepan. Heat to boiling, reduce the heat and simmer to reduce and thicken. Use this to baste the turkey during the last 30 minutes of cooking. Allow the breast to rest at room temperature for 15 minutes before carving.

Chicken on the Mediterranean

2 tsp. of olive oil

4 boneless chicken breasts

3 cloves chopped garlic

3 cups diced tomatoes

½ cup diced onions

½ cup good cooking white wine

Fresh thyme

Fresh basil

Fresh parsley

½ cup black olives

Heat the oil and 2 tablespoons white wine in a large skillet over medium heat. Cook chicken about 4 to 6 minutes each side, until golden. Remove chicken from skillet and set aside.

Sauté garlic and onion in pan drippings Add tomatoes and bring to a boil. Lower heat, add 1/2 cup white wine and simmer for 10 minutes. Add thyme and basil and simmer for 5 more minutes.

Return chicken to skillet and cover. Cook over low heat until the chicken is cooked through and no longer pink inside. Add olives and parsley to the skillet and cook for 1 minute. Season with salt and pepper to taste and serve.

Linguini with Garlic

1 10oz. package of linguini pasta

2 tbsp. olive oil

Minced garlic, oregano, thyme, and basil (2 tablespoons each or to preferred taste)

2 cups chopped tomatoes (cherry, roma, your choice)

Cook pasta in a large pot of boiling water until done. Drain.

Meanwhile, heat oil in large saucepan. Add garlic and cook for 2 minutes, stirring constantly. Crush herbs and add to the garlic then add in the linguine. Heat through stirring frequently. Fold in tomatoes.

Black Bean and Rice Bake

cups cooked rice (brown preferred)

bouillon cube (vegetable, chicken or beef)

Juice from 1/2 lime

can of black beans (rinsed and drained)

bag of spinach (baby or regular)

garlic clove (minced)

10 oz package of frozen corn

scallions or green onion (chop coarsely)

medium zucchini (grated while raw)

.5 cups of salsa

cups diced tomatoes (roughly 1 large can or fresh)

cups of cheddar cheese (grate)

tablespoon parsley (minced)

Begin by preheating your oven to 350 degrees.

Cook rice as per the directions on the package and then add the bouillon cube to the water while it cooks. When done, let the rice sit covered for 10 minutes. After rice has cooled, fluff and toss with the fresh lime juice.

Move the rice to a large bowl. Rinse and drain the black beans and add to the rice.

Sauté the spinach with the minced garlic in a little olive oil until slightly wilted. Add this to the rice and beans, folding together gently.

Sauté the corn and scallions in the same pan and cook over medium heat for 3 minutes. Add the corn and scallions to the bowl.

Grate the zucchini in raw form and add to bowl (this will cook easily in the oven and does not need to be cooked ahead of time).

Add the salsa to the bowl along with the diced tomatoes. If you use canned tomatoes, you can include the juice from the can as well or otherwise add ¼ cup of water to the mixture. Add 1 cup of grated cheese to the bowl then mix everything together in the bowl.

Lightly grease a 10 x 8 casserole dish. Pour the whole mixture into the casserole pan. Top with the remaining 1 cup of grated cheese then bake in the oven for 40 minutes.

Remove and sprinkle minced parsley over the top to finish.

Orange-Mint Lamb Chops

4 teaspoons olive oil, divided

2 teaspoons grated orange rind

1 tablespoon freshly squeezed orange juice

1/4 cup fresh mint (chop coarsely)

8 (4-ounce) lamb rib chops (trim off excess fat)

1 teaspoon salt

1/2 teaspoon freshly ground black pepper

Cooking spray (ideally with an olive oil base)

3 tablespoons balsamic vinegar

Combine 1 tablespoon olive oil, orange rind, and juice in a large, sealable plastic bag. Add the lamb chops to the bag and ensure all of the chops are coated well. Let marinate at room temperature for 10 minutes. Remove lamb from bag, sprinkle evenly with salt and pepper and heat in a large frying pan over medium heat. Spray the pan with cooking spray before frying. Cook for 2 minutes on each side (or more if you prefer it more well-done).

Place the vinegar in a small skillet over medium-high heat; bring to a boil. Cook 3 minutes or until vinegar becomes thick like syrup. Drizzle the vinegar and remaining 1 teaspoon of olive oil over the lamb and serve.

You can choose a simple green salad to accompany these chops or you can choose one of the salad selections from Chapter 4 to make a memorable meal.

Veggie and Halloumi Kebabs

For the veggie kebabs:

12 white or cremini mushrooms (clean and remove stems)

12 cherry tomatoes

1 zucchini (cut into 1/2-inch chunks)

1 of each medium-large red and yellow bell peppers

3 cups of yellow squash (cut into 1/2-inch chunks)

12 ounces halloumi cheese (cut into 1/2-inch squares)

Have 12 skewers on hand to prepare the kebabs

For the marinade sauce:

1/2 cup balsamic or red wine vinegar

1/2 cup extra virgin olive oil (high grade)

3 tablespoons honey

3 tablespoons Dijon mustard

2 1/2 tablespoons fresh basil (chopped finely)

3 cloves garlic (minced)

1/2 teaspoon salt

1/2 teaspoon freshly ground black pepper

Preheat a BBQ or grill to medium-high heat.

For the sauce, place the vinegar, olive oil, honey, mustard, basil, garlic, salt and pepper in a small bowl and whisk together.

To make the kebabs, simply place the mushrooms, tomatoes, zucchini, peppers and squash in a plastic bag and pour the marinade sauce over. Mix around the sauce so the veggies are all coated for best grilling results. Marinate for 3 to 4 hours in the bag, occasionally turning over to ensure sauce soaks into all parts.

Remove the vegetables from the marinade sauce pouch, saving any leftover marinade to be used later. Arrange as you wish, making sure that each skewer has the full variety of veggies (except the tomatoes and cheese). Place the kebabs with the mushrooms, zucchini, squash and peppers on the grill first as they take longer to cook and soften. Grill until the vegetables have cooked which takes approximately 10-15 minutes at medium heat. Place the cherry tomatoes and halloumi cheese on skewers (rotating between the two) and grill for 4 minutes.

Once the vegetables are cooked, you can serve as is on the skewer or you can remove from the skewer and place together in a bowl if you wish. Then add in the leftover marinade from before and toss together. Serve with your preferred side dishes or offer as an appetizer with your favorite dips.

Chapter 10: For Your Sweet Tooth

Frosty Banana Smoothie with Almond Milk

1/3 cup chopped pitted dates

2 tablespoons warm water

2 cups vanilla almond milk, chilled

1/2 cup fat-free vanilla soy or dairy yogurt

1 very ripe banana, frozen earlier without the peeling

4 ice cubes

1/8 teaspoon ground nutmeg, plus extra for garnish

Put the dates in a small bowl and sprinkle with the warm water. Let soak for five minutes to soften, and drain.

In a blender, combine the dates, almond milk, yogurt, banana, ice cubes and the 1/8 teaspoon nutmeg. Blend until smooth and frothy, about 30 seconds.

Pour into chilled glasses. Serves four.

Zesty Poached Pears

1 cup orange juice

1/4 cup apple juice

1 teaspoon ground cinnamon

1 teaspoon ground nutmeg

4 whole pears

1/2 cup fresh raspberries

2 tablespoons orange zest

In a small bowl, combine the juices, cinnamon, and nutmeg.

Peel the pears and leave the stems. Remove the core from the bottom of the pear. Place in a shallow pan. Add the juice mixture to the pan and set over medium heat. Simmer for about 30 minutes carefully turning pears frequently.

Garnish the pears with raspberries and orange zest and serve immediately. Serves four.

Orange Ricotta Cake

3 pounds or roughly 5 1/2 cups of fresh ricotta cheese

8 large eggs

1/2 pound or roughly 1 cup of brown sugar

Zest of one orange (wash first)

Zest of one lemon (wash first)

Butter for coating the pan

Preheat the oven to 425 degrees.

In a large bowl, mix all the ingredients together very well.

Apply the butter in a thin coat to the bottom and sides of a 9" spring form pan. Pour the mix into the greased pan then bake for 30 minutes at 425 degrees. Reduce the over heat to 380 degrees and continue baking for an additional 40 minutes.

Let it cool and serve.

Fruit Salad with Greek Yogurt

3 small oranges (peel, remove seed and cut into small pieces)

3 cups grapes (seedless, cut in half)

2 cups fresh apricots (remove pit and cut into 4)

3 small peaches (remove pit and cut into small cubes)

1 cup sliced almonds (raw or roasted are fine)

4 cups Balkan-style yogurt

4 tablespoons of honey

This recipe is fresh and simple. Prepare these typical Mediterranean fruits as defined above. Toss together in a large bowl. You can either place 1/2 cup to 1 cup of yogurt into each bowl and place an equal amount of fruit on top or you can mix the fruit and yogurt together in the bowl. Once dished up, add 1-2 tablespoons of sliced almonds to each serving and drizzle honey over top.

Rice Pudding

1 cup coconut milk (about 1/2 can)

1 tablespoon honey

1 cup cooked brown or white rice

Dash of cinnamon and nutmeg

This simple recipe makes four small servings or two large ones. Begin by pouring the coconut milk into a small pot over medium-high heat. Bring to a simmer. Add the honey and stir to combine. Add in the rice and continue to stir until evenly mixed together.

Let mixture simmer for about 5 minutes. Bring it to a boil, and the water will evaporate making the mixture to become thicker. Cook until you reach the desired consistency, but keep a close watch as the liquid cooks off. When serving, sprinkle with cinnamon and nutmeg, and you can add drizzle some honey on top.

Panna Cotta

1 gelatin packet (2 1/4 teaspoons)

8 ounces of heavy cream

1 liter (17.6 ounces) of Greek yogurt (vanilla flavor works well, but you may choose your preferred flavor)

1/3 cup white sugar

1 tablespoon vanilla extract

Toppings: apricots, strawberries, raspberries, blueberries, cherries or some combination often works well. Nuts or chocolate (sauce or shavings) can also be a more decadent addition.

In a small bowl containing 2 tablespoons of water, sprinkle the gelatin and let soak for five minutes.

While this is congealing, bring the cream, sugar and vanilla to a gentle simmer in a small saucepan while stirring constantly. Turn off the heat and let it cool for one minute.

The gelatin should now be one congealed piece. Transfer it into the saucepan with the cream and sugar mixture (not on the heat, only after the mixture has cooled for one minute).

In a large mixing bowl, whisk the Greek yogurt until it is smooth and free of any lumps. Add in the cream mixture slowly as you continue to whisk gently.

Pour it into roughly 1/2 cup portions into dessert cups and refrigerate for 3 or more hours (until it has set into a solid form). When ready, added your toppings and serve chilled.

Grilled Peaches with Sweet Cheese Sauce

2 tablespoons light brown sugar

1/2 teaspoon cinnamon

4 fresh peaches (remove pit and cut into 1/4 inch thick slices)

2 tablespoons of grapeseed or canola oil (or other vegetable oil with a mild flavor)

For the sauce:

8 ounces of low-fat cream cheese (softened in the microwave for 20 seconds)

1 liter (8 ounces) low-fat yogurt (plain or vanilla flavored)

1/4 cup packed brown or golden sugar

1 teaspoon vanilla extract

2 tablespoons milk

To prepare the peaches:

In a small bowl, combine the brown sugar and cinnamon. Cut the peaches into slices discarding the pits. Use the grapeseed oil (slightly warmed so it is easy to work with) to brush the peach slices all over, coating all sides completely. Place the peaches on a hot grill until fruit has grill marks on each side (which takes roughly 3 minutes for a side. Sprinkle the peaches with cinnamon sugar while still on the grill. Cover the grill and cook until sugar melts and fruit is tender, about 10 to 15 minutes.

To prepare the sauce:

Place the softened cream cheese in your mixing bowl and beat on low speed until creamy and smooth. Slowly add the yogurt and continue to beat until well combined. Then add the brown sugar and vanilla and beat until fully combined (and consistent). Using a spoon stir in enough milk to reach desired consistency to drizzle or put a dollop over the grilled peaches. To thicken, cover and let sit in the fridge for 1 to 2 hours.

Almond Flour Cookies

1/2 teaspoon sea salt

1/2 teaspoon baking soda

2 cups blanched almond flour

1/4 cup dried cranberries (unsweetened for a healthier option)

1/2 cup dried apricots (cut into small pieces, 6 per apricot)

1/4 cup sunflower seeds (without shells)

1/4 cup raw sesame seeds

1/4 cup pistachios (chop coarsely)

1 large egg

2 tablespoons honey

Preheat the oven to 350 degrees.

Combine the salt, baking soda and almond flour thoroughly in a large mixing bowl. Stir in the dried fruit, seeds and nuts until all are connected well into the batter.

In a small bowl combine the large egg and the honey.

Knead together, the wet ingredients into the dry gently and thoroughly.

Use your hands to form dough so all of the pieces are held in the batter securely. Press the mixture into small cookies roughly 1.5 inches in diameter and 3/4 inch thick (about 1/4 cup each).

Lay the cookies a baking sheet lined with parchment paper for 10-12 minutes so they can cool. Serve warm or slightly cooled for a harder consistency.

Halva

1 1/4 cups honey

1 cup light tahini paste (stirred well to mix in any excess oil)

Begin by lining the base and sides of a baking tin with parchment paper.

Place the honey in a medium saucepan on a high heat and bring to a boil. Continue to boil for 8–10 minutes, stirring regularly.

To test if the honey is ready, simply place a spoonful in a small bowl of cold water and as it cools, it will form a soft ball. If it does not do this, the remaining mixture needs to stay on the heat for another 1-2 minutes.

Once finished heating the honey, cool for 3 minutes off of the heat. Now stir in the tahini paste and pour into the tin lined with parchment.

Continue to cool, then cover and place in the fridge. Leave to sit for 36 hours to allow it to set properly. The texture needs time to form. Once the texture is achieved, slice into slabs to serve.

Pasteli

1 1/2 cup sesame seeds

1/2 cup honey

1 teaspoon butter or canola oil

Toast the sesame seeds in a dry pan until they slightly brown (but not too much).

Pour the honey into medium saucepan and heat the honey until it starts to bubble a medium-high heat.

Pour in the toasted sesame seeds then lower the heat and stir. Heat the mixture for about 5-10 minutes.

Line a pan with slightly greased wax paper (using butter or canola oil) and pour in the mixture. For a flat bar, place another sheet of wax paper on top of what was just poured in and spread out the sesame-honey mix with a rolling pin. You may choose to make a very thin sheet or leave it a little thicker.

Remove the top sheet carefully and let it cool for about 15 minutes. Cut into small strips using a sharp knife or a pizza cutter and serve as bars.

Let them cool completely. Store in an airtight container with wax paper between the layers of bars so they do not stick together.

Chapter 11: Snacking Like a Star

When you transition from a predominantly processed diet rich in sugar and preservatives, to one that uses mainly fresh ingredients, you may find yourself wanting to eat more regularly. This is often because the same quantity of the fresh food would have fewer calories than the processed one. For example, a 100g apple compared to a 100g chocolate bar has roughly 400 calories less. So it is very normal for your body to crave for a snack after a shorter amount of time while you switch over to a new way of eating and living. Don't worry. You will not end up being malnourished, nor would you starve. Nuts, oils, and cheese provide a great balance to your low calorie, high fiber options. They will help you feel full longer while providing your body the necessary micronutrients that help heal the body and keep the mind strong.

Having a snack mid-morning, mid-afternoon and in the evening is common and acceptable. Over time, however, you may find yourself more and more satisfied with three main meals per day and desiring snacks between meals less and less. Plus, by adding more fresh fruits and vegetables, you are adding more fiber and creating a healthier digestive system. Your body will quickly move to a new way of processing food and will use what you consume. This "new normal" will mean more energy and fewer cravings for unhealthy foods without even having to engage your willpower.

When thinking about the best approach to snacking on the Mediterranean Diet, think fresh first. If the food you want to snack on closely resembles how it came out of the earth or off the tree, then you can assume it is a good snack decision. This means fruits, vegetables and nuts are a mainstay in Mediterranean snacking. Beyond that, meats and cheeses in reasonable portions can also help you stave off hunger and hold you over until the next meal.

Examples of good snacks:

- 1/4 cup cashews

- 1 small apple

- Citrus fruit (orange or grapefruit)

- 2 hardboiled eggs

- Carrots with cheese slices

- Sliced apple with 2 tablespoons nut butter

- 1/2 cup Trail mix with raw nuts and dried fruits

- 1/2 cup roasted pumpkin or sunflower seeds with spices and a dash of salt

- 1/2 cup roasted chickpeas with garlic powder

- 1 Cup raw veggie sticks (cucumbers, carrots, celery) with 2 tablespoons hummus

- 1 Cup low-fat yogurt with 1/2 fruit

- 1 slice whole grain toast with nut butter

- 2 rice cakes with 1/2 cup tuna

- Fruit smoothie with almond milk or yogurt

- Unsweetened applesauce

- 1/2 cup berries with 1/2 cup low fat cottage cheese

- 1/4 avocado on 6 whole grain crackers

- 4 slices of deli meat with 4 thin slices of cheese (make roll ups with both together)

- Smoked salmon and light cream cheese on 2 slices of whole wheat baguette

- 1/2 cup granola with ½ cup low fat yogurt

- Turkey, salmon or beef jerky (2 pieces, low salt)

- 6 olives with 2 slices of feta cheese

- 2 cups of air popped popcorn

- 1 cup natural, low sugar frozen yogurt

- 1/2 baked sweet potato with 2 tablespoons of feta

If you fear leaving behind your old snacking habits, check out these alternatives that will help you switch up to better quality snacking foods, but satisfy your cravings for sweet, salty, crunch or flavorful foods.

If you like:

Chips, pretzels or crackers

Now try:

Carrots, celery, broccoli with yogurt dip or salsa

If you like:

Ice cream

Now try:

Low fat, low sugar frozen yogurt or a fresh fruit smoothie made with Greek yogurt

If you like:

Banana split

Now try:

Grilled banana drizzled with honey and almond slivers sprinkled on top

If you like:

Nachos covered in cheese

Now try:

A few multigrain crackers with light cheese

If you like:

French fries and ketchup

Now try:

Baked sweet potato fries with tzatziki dip made with yogurt

If you like:

Popcorn smothered in butter and salt

Now try:

Air-popped popcorn with a light spray of extra virgin olive oil and a dash of herbs

If you like:

Candy

Now try:

Dried fruit or trail mix (this is still high calorie, so consume this in moderation and be sure to get an unsweetened version)

If you like:

Cheesecake

Now try:

Low-fat vanilla yogurt topped with fruit

If you like:

High sugar sodas

Now try:

Chilled herbal tea

If you like:

Beer

Now try:

Red wine (1 glass recommended per day)

If you like nuts and seeds and want to expand beyond the typical almonds, cashews and sunflower seeds found in most snack recipes, consider some of the following:

- Black walnut

- Brazil nut

- Chia seeds

- Chestnuts

- Chinese almond

- Earth almond

- Earth nut

- English walnuts

- Filbert

- Flax seeds

- Gingko nut

- Hazelnut

- Hemp seeds

- Japanese walnut

- Juniper Berry

- Macadamia

- Oak acorns

- Pecan

- Persian walnuts

- Pili nut

- Pine nut

- Pistachio

- Poppy seeds

- Pumpkin seeds

- Sesame seeds

- Safflower seeds

- Tiger nut

- Walnut

- White nut

- White walnut

If you like the idea of veggies as a snack or veggies and dip (hummus, bean, nut butter yogurt or cheese-based dips), consider the array of different vegetables to draw from:

- Artichoke

- Arugula

- Asparagus

- Beets

- Beetroot

- Bok Choy

- Broccoflower (a hybrid)

- Broccoli

- Brussels sprouts

- Cabbage

- Calabrese

- Carrots

- Cauliflower

- Celery

- Chard

- Collard greens

- Corn

- Cucumber

- Endive

- Fiddleheads

- Fennel

- Kale

- Kohlrabi

- Lettuce

- Mushrooms (actually a fungus, not a plant but taxes as a vegetable)

- Mustard greens

- Okra

- Onion (and related vegetables in the onion family)

- Peppers (sweet, bell, spicy)

- Potato (many varieties)

- Pumpkin

- Rhubarb

- Radish

- Spinach

- Squash

- Sweet potato

- Taro

- Turnip

- Water chestnut

- Watercress

- Zucchini

For fruits, just think every color of the rainbow. Variety is key. You can eat your fruit simple and whole. You could also make it into a fruit salad or a puree to change things up. Further, you can add a low-fat yogurt to keep things interesting. Here are some fruits to consider to keep your diet varied and fresh:

- Apple

- Apricot

- Avocado

- Banana

- Bilberry
- Blackberry
- Blackcurrant
- Blueberry
- Boysenberry
- Cantaloupe
- Currant
- Cherry
- Cherimoya
- Cloudberry
- Coconut
- Cranberry
- Date
- Dragonfruit
- Durian
- Elderberry
- Fig
- Goji berry
- Gooseberry
- Grape
- Grapefruit
- Guava
- Huckleberry

- Jackfruit

- Juniper Berry

- Kiwifruit

- Kumquat

- Lemon

- Lime

- Loquat

- Lychee

- Mango

- Melon

- Cantaloupe

- Honeydew

- Watermelon

- Miracle fruit

- Mulberry

- Nectarine

- Orange (many varieties: blood, clementine, mandarin, tangerine)

- Papaya

- Passionfruit

- Peach

- Pear

- Persimmon

- Physalis

- Plantain

- Plum/prune (dried plum)

- Pineapple

- Pomegranate

- Pomelo

- Raspberry

- Rambutan

- Satsuma (similar to an orange)

- Starfruit

- Strawberry

If you want to add a little additional protein to any fruit or veggie snack, consider adding a small amount of cheese. This can help address hunger if you find you are not completely satisfied with just fruit and vegetables. If you have enough mozzarella, cheddar in your diet, consider some alternatives:

- Asiago

- Blue

- Brie

- Camembert

- Canadian cheddar

- Capricorn goat

- Colby-Jack

- Cornish pepper

- Crema Mexicana

- Edam
- Feta
- Four herb gouda
- Gorgonzola
- Gouda
- Gruyère
- Haloumi-style
- Havarti
- Marble cheddar
- Monterey jack
- Monterey jack dry
- Paneer
- Pepper jack
- Provolone
- Queso jalapeno
- Ricotta
- Roquefort
- String
- Swiss
- Swiss
- White cheddar

These lists will be helpful to review when you want to keep your diet interesting. When you want to try something new or sprout a new snack idea, come here for ideas. Beyond these examples, consider small portions of other Mediterranean meals such as salads, meats, and grilled vegetables. Preparing to have the right snacks on hand can be easy if you simply pack up a small portion of leftovers to grab when hunger strikes between meals.

Chapter 12: Meal Planning Made Easy

Meal planning can be very easy after only a couple of weeks of trying recipes and reading about this diet. You will quickly see what is included and what can be eaten in moderation. Soon enough, it will be intuitive for you in determining what to buy, make and consume.

Start by thinking in broad strokes about the foods that you have a full green light to consume, those that can be consumed but to a lesser degree (yellow light) and those to avoid (red light).

Green light: Vegetables (including potatoes), legumes, fruits, nuts, seeds, whole grains, bread, herbs, spices, fish, seafood and extra virgin olive oil.

Yellow light: Poultry, eggs, red meat, cheese, red wine and yogurt.

Red light: Sugar-sweetened beverages, candy, products with added sugars, products with trans-fats (including deep fried foods), processed meats, refined grains, refined oils and other highly processed foods.

If you would prefer to think about the diet in terms of a timeline, consider the foods you can aim to eat daily and those that should be reserved for a weekly or monthly schedule. Daily you can consume rice, couscous, grains, potatoes, olive oil, vegetables, fruits, beans, legumes, nuts, cheese, yogurt and one glass of red wine. Weekly you can consume fish, poultry, eggs and some sweets. Weekly would mean an indulgence once or twice a week but not daily. Red meat should be consumed once a month or so, and if you can help it, even less frequently.

That should help you define the main principles. Selecting recipes from the previous chapters can make the learning curve quite painless as well, and certainly fun. You can select from breakfasts, mains, salads, snacks and you can even find recipes for desserts if you have a sweet tooth (of course sugar is always used in moderation in this lifestyle).

In terms of what to drink, make water your primary beverage when on the Mediterranean diet. Many are pleased to find that this diet also includes moderate amounts of red wine. One glass per day is considered reasonable. This matches with the social component of this lifestyle. Picture people gathered around the kitchen, cooking and sipping wine. You also have the green light for coffee and teas, but avoid high-fat creams, sugar, and artificial sweeteners. Also, avoid both regular and low-calorie sodas, sugar-sweetened juices and anything else with either a high amount of added sugar or synthetic or highly processed sweetener alternatives.

If it helps to have it all spelled out for you while you are still getting used to the lifestyle, find below a sample meal plan for two weeks to get you started.

Week 1

Monday

Breakfast: Greek yogurt with sliced fruits and a handful of nuts

Lunch: Chicken breast wrap with a side green salad

Dinner: Broiled salmon with brown rice and grilled vegetables

Tuesday

Breakfast: Scrambled eggs and grilled vegetables (cook with olive oil)

Lunch: Greek yogurt with peaches and granola (add nuts if you would like)

Dinner: Grilled lamb chops, with couscous salad and baked sweet potato

Wednesday

Breakfast: Oatmeal with raisins or currants, almonds, and an apple chopped up (add a tablespoon of honey on top if desired)

Lunch: Whole grain sandwich with avocado, Dijon mustard, and sliced turkey

Dinner: Mediterranean pizza (crust made with whole wheat flour), topped with mozzarella and feta cheese, vegetables and black olives

Thursday

Breakfast: Greek yogurt with berries and 1/2 cup granola or oats

Lunch: Whole grain wrap with grilled eggplant and zucchini, with a slice of provolone

Dinner: A green salad topped with tuna, dressed with olive oil, fresh herbs and added spices. Cup of fruit salad for dessert

Friday

Breakfast: Oatmeal with raisins and honey

Lunch: Quinoa salad with spinach and chickpeas

Dinner: Salad with plenty of greens, tomatoes, olives and feta cheese. Baked apple for dessert

Saturday

Breakfast: Omelet with tomatoes and onions and a side of fruit salad

Lunch: Whole grain sandwich with cheese and fresh vegetables

Dinner: Mediterranean lasagne with eggplant, zucchini, sweet potatoes, tomatoes and shrimp

Sunday

Breakfast: Egg white omelet with spinach and olives

Lunch: Whole grain wrap with lettuce, hummus, tomatoes and black beans

Dinner: Grilled chicken breast with vegetables and a baked potato with fruit for dessert

Week 2

Monday

Breakfast: Egg white omelet with spinach and feta cheese, piece of fruit

Lunch: Chickpea and Couscous salad on a bed of greens, topped with nuts

Dinner: Grilled chicken breast with quinoa and steamed vegetables

Tuesday

Breakfast: Greek yogurt with granola and apple

Lunch: Black bean wrap with tomatoes and avocado, with dollop of Greek yogurt and spice

Dinner: Seafood stir fry with vegetables and a side of whole grain pasta

Wednesday

Breakfast: Hardboiled eggs on whole grain toast with cheese and tomatoes

Lunch: Lentils and brown rice on baby spinach

Dinner: Grilled salmon with carrots and sweet potatoes

Thursday

Breakfast: Greek yogurt with berries and 1/2 cup granola or oats

Lunch: Wrap with almond butter and slices of pears and strawberries, cup of yogurt on the side with nuts and honey

Dinner: Vegetable frittata with a side of green salad topped with pine nuts and white beans

Friday

Breakfast: Oatmeal with peaches, granola, and honey

Lunch: Spinach salad with berries, ricotta cheese, and olive oil vinaigrette

Dinner: Seafood linguine in red sauce with squash and zucchini, small treat for dessert (sweet)

Saturday

Breakfast: Whole wheat crepes (low sugar) with fresh fruit, Greek yogurt and honey

Lunch: Greek salad with cucumbers, onions, tomatoes, feta, spices, olive oil with whole grain pita and hummus on the side

Dinner: Flatbread pizzas with sun-dried tomatoes, fresh tomatoes, olives, spinach, artichokes, mozzarella with a side of fresh fruit

Sunday

Breakfast: Scrambled eggs served on toast with lettuce and tomato

Lunch: Pasta salad with loads of fresh vegetables and a dash of romano cheese

Dinner: Lamb kebabs with a side of grilled eggplant parmesan and rice

When you plan your shopping trips, think about spending the majority of time in the produce area. Vegetables are the foundation of the diet. Go for lots of different colors and be sure to stock up on leafy greens as well as fresh herbs. Your next priority is fruit, so everything from citrus to berries and apples should be considered. Follow that up by selecting legumes, nuts, fish, seafood and good cuts of lean meat. Dairy such as Greek yogurt and light cheeses are next. Whole grains, bread and pastas can be added next. Don't forget your extra virgin olive oil and spices to round everything out.

There is a great deal of flexibility with this diet as you can see. This means that you can substitute seafood for legumes or spinach for sweet potatoes. You have the ability to cater to you and your families likes and dislikes easily. If you observe the essence of this diet, you will quickly make it your own and establish your favorite recipes while still leaving yourself lots of room to experiment.

Chapter 13: Mistakes and Misconceptions

Whenever a new concept becomes popular, for instance, a diet, there are lots of rumors and misconceptions. There are also lots of people who adopt it without researching it much, and then complain that the diet does not work for one reason or another. This chapter is intended to dispel the myths so you can get a clarity about what to expect, what to avoid and what is just plain malarkey.

As humans, we find it extremely difficult to give up old habits. We seek out the exceptions and loopholes, where we can work around the rules in order to have it all. Of course, we soon find ourselves wondering why we are not getting the results the diet promises. The Mediterranean Diet is flexible and full of variety, so this instinct is not elicited in the same way as with other, more restrictive diets. It is intended to provide a feasible and appealing lifestyle change that can be sustained over time, so it is not about a hasty race to the bottom (the bottom of the scale that is). That said, it is helpful to be aware of where a new dieter can go wrong so you can plan better and avoid these common mistakes.

Mistake #1: Pasta and bread are Mediterranean, and they will make me thin and energized - the more, the better

Even when you read the above phrase, it is probably challenging to buy really into it, even for a second. Although it may be obviously false, a lot of people want to turn up the white carbohydrates and turn down the veggies and legumes. This is likely due to old habits re-emerging. People do not want to give up comfort food and convenience foods. They think the only way to be full is to stuff themselves with pasta. Your body will probably adjust to the new way of eating much faster than your brain. So you may have the urge to polish off a whole baguette at the beginning before you become accustomed to eating more veggies and less wheat-based carbohydrates. Bread and pasta are an integral part of this diet. They need be consumed a bit less than what you are used to, daily. Moderation is key. Vegetables, legumes, nuts, olive oil, and fruits should comprise the majority of your daily consumption plan, but a slice of whole grain bread or a cup of pasta with supper is absolutely acceptable. Just don't make them the foundation or you will soon find yourself disappointed with your results and resorting to other bad habits too.

Mistake #2: Eating out at all of your favorite Mediterranean restaurants as much as you want

The principles of the diet that center around fresh foods, good oils, less animal products and whole grains are seen at times on restaurant menus. However, for the most part, restaurants want you coming back for their delectable foods, so they do not shy away from adding more fat, sugar, salt and carbohydrates than traditionally seen in this cuisine. Heaping plates of pasta, tons of full-fat cheeses and red meat are okay now and then. They are not okay every day or even every week. It should be an occasional experience. Also, remember that this diet is espousing a lifestyle that is more mindful and involves you preparing your foods, so eating at restaurants really only tackles the food part of it; and it may not do such a good job at that in the end. Remember, the diet is also about how you eat your food and not just what you eat. If you happen to find a great Mediterranean salad at a restaurant, you do not need to shy away from eating there. If you find healthy options that are also convenient when you need food prepared for you, go for it. But it would be a mistake to think that any restaurant serving Mediterranean food will meet your new diet and lifestyle targets.

Mistake #3: Bring on the red wine!

Red wine is unmistakably part of this diet. A glass per day is part of the dietary and social aspects of this lifestyle. In this case, more of a good thing is not considered better. One glass is the right amount to reap the health benefits of red wine without crossing over into the realm of increased health risks. Feeling drowsy or dehydrated as a result of polishing off a bottle, not to mention the additional calories, will have your good eating negated. Stick to one glass.

Mistake #4: Just change what you eat and expect to lose weight

There is no question that increasing fruit and vegetable intake will bring a plethora of health benefits from feeling more energized to sleeping better and having better digestion. Ditching hydrogenated oils for extra virgin olive oil can help your cardiovascular health and stave off lots of long-term health problems. However, the eating aspect of the lifestyle is not the place to stop. Another key component is being physically active - walking, biking, doing light exercise daily. This will make a significant difference in terms of any weight-related goals you have. It's also true to the Mediterranean lifestyle the diet was founded on where people would walk everyday, run their errands on foot and scale hills in the process. Honor this aspect of the lifestyle and you will be pleased.

Mistake #5: Go full out with cheese

Cheese and dairy were and still are a regular part of the Mediterranean diet. They are second to all things fresh from the earth. Fruits, veggies, legumes and nuts are all prioritized over cheese and dairy in this diet. Cheese is a great complement to any healthy dish, but it is intended to be consumed in moderation. You should keep in mind that high-fat dairy products are less ideal than the low fat alternatives. Highly processed foods, especially those with artificial sweeteners are not a part of this diet though. This means that you shouldn't be looking to trade out quality, yet high-fat alternatives for dairy products that claim to be 'diet' but contain a lot of sugar or artificial sweeteners. Stick with a high quality, even if a high fat product, but consume it in moderation to complement the mainstays of the diet like vegetables and fish.

Mistake #6: Plan to take on this diet for the short term only

This is not a crash diet. It will not get you extreme results as compared to a very restrictive diet intended for weight loss at any cost. This is a lifestyle shift that will spell great long term health as well a strong and lean body. That said, if you are currently overweight, you will shed pounds gradually over time. If you maintain this lifestyle, you will get results and maintain them. However, if you're looking for fast results, there may be more direct, albeit riskier routes, to getting there. So manage your expectations that this is a lifestyle shift. You will feel great. You will get results. And you will maintain your results over time. You will probably also report a better quality of life satisfaction overall and appreciate the social and the physical aspects of this lifestyle as well.

If you take this awareness of common mistakes and translate it into thoughtful action, you will be sure to reap the benefits of this diet without falling into any traps. Soon enough, your knowledge of the diet will turn into a habit. You will not have to be so considered about what to pursue versus avoid. You will fall into natural behavior while shopping, planning, and cooking.

Misconceptions abound with the Mediterranean Diet. Although the principles of the diet are simple, straightforward and easy to follow, myths continue to float around.

Misconception #1: Consuming fat will make me fat

You have probably noticed by now that the Mediterranean Diet uses olive oil regularly and promotes the consumption of nuts and seeds. These are excellent sources of fat, better than lower quality oils, saturated fats and hydrogenated oils. Fats are, without question, a calorie-dense source of nutrition. So you will not see proponents of the diet recommending consuming a cup of olive oil per day while also promising you a weight loss. You see a tablespoon recommended here and there. You will also hear people recommending to prioritize using olive oil over other oils, as the best choice. Fat is not metabolized in the body in a way that leads directly to fat production and storage. It is used like any other building block of cells and the metabolic process to provide energy, to facilitate healing and to maintain vital bodily function. This means that if you have a balanced diet consisting of vegetables, fruits, fish, legumes, lean meats, light dairy, and olive oil, you can maintain a healthy weight without storing extra fat.

Misconception #2: This diet will cost me a lot of money

When you first take a glance at the prices in the organic aisle, you might find yourself worrying about your budget. This is natural. At first review, you might think it would be easy to spend a lot more money if you switch to consuming more natural, mostly fresh foods. You are not absurd for making this initial assessment. That said, in short order you will become savvy at deciding how to spend your hard-earned dollars and your money might even stretch further than before. We often think of processed foods as being convenient and we forget that not only is there a cost to our health, but often a financial price tag as well. For example, if you compare a box of frozen processed fish sticks with purchasing fresh fillets, the price difference is comparable but the quality of the fresh fish is remarkably different. If you're comparing crackers and processed wheat-based products to purchasing rice or couscous, you will actually end up saving money. Keep in mind you will be eating more reasonable portions of food as well so it is not always a gram per gram comparison.

Buying seasonally can help. Buying root vegetables, squash and pumpkins in the autumn and buying berries in the summer can help you with costs too. You can buy direct from farmers at markets or roadside where possible. You will also see a marked change in prices in conventional grocery stores depending on the growing season. Pay attention to these trends and consider eating more seasonally to keep costs down and quality up.

As you become more intentional about your meals and even do some meal planning, you will find there is a lot less food going to waste. You end up purchasing the things you need and there will be nothing rotting in the back of your fridge.

Misconception #3: I won't feel sated by this diet

With any transition in eating, you may experience cravings for food you no longer eat. That is completely normal. Sometimes this is mistaken for a listless hunger, but often it's simply the brain transitioning to a new way of doing things. Your habits, through your neural pathways, still want you to continue your old behaviors, but this will fade over time. Whenever someone is shifting from high-calorie convenience foods to lower calorie natural foods, they will inevitably crave their old habits. Those processed foods are designed to give us a quick good feeling. We should not give in to the temptation and avoid the aftereffects of consuming fast food. We should simply stick to the wisdom that these new food choices will serve us better in the short and long terms. Especially during the initial period of switching to the Mediterranean Diet, be sure to increase your water intake. This will make a big difference in cutting through cravings that spur from leaving behind old food choices.

If you find yourself still wanting after just finishing a meal or waking up hungry, you might want to look at the balance of what you are eating. Start by reflecting on your protein intake. Consuming protein can help you maintain a feeling of being full for longer. This does not mean you have to switch back to a routine of consuming red meat at each meal. Look at options like fish, seafood, lentils, beans and dairy products. All of these are high in protein and should do the trick.

Beyond water and protein, you can consider slightly increasing your quality or amount of grain products. Start by looking at whole grain options which take longer to digest such as brown rice and quinoa. These are great alternatives that will fill you up more easily than a white pasta alternative for example. The old expression 'they will stick to your ribs' references the ability for foods like whole grains and oatmeal to stay with you longer and rid you of that quick regression back to hunger. So once you have addressed the quality issue, you should find a marked decrease in that sense that you need more food. If you don't, then look at your portion sizes. If you increase your portions by half a cup during your transition phase (and eventually reduce back to smaller portions), you may be able to help yourself stay on this new diet while addressing the urge to consume more.

Snacking is another part of your diet you might adjust in order to deal with that sense that you are not full. Your meals might be a good size and quality, but you may still need something to hold you over between meals. Snacking is acceptable on this diet. Review the chapter on snacking for suggestions. If you carry a piece of fruit such as an apple or orange with you, you may be able to quickly handle your hunger without making far worse choices at a convenience store or drive thru.

With the Mediterranean lifestyle comes a practice of eating more mindfully. This means eating without the distraction of a cell phone or television. When we eat with attention to our every mouthful, we more fully experience our food. Research shows that people also eat less when eating without technology. When you take on this facet of the diet, you will likely find you achieve your satiation level much sooner than normal. The simple process of being able to account for every bite as well as slowing down your eating will snap you out of a post-meal hunt for more food.

Misconception #4: A vegetarian cannot go on this diet

For whatever reason someone chooses to be a vegetarian, this diet can be for you. As you read through the inclusion and exclusions in this diet, you might find that vegetarians are very well-suited to this lifestyle. Fresh fruits and vegetables, grains, nuts and legumes are the mainstay of this diet. That fits a vegan or vegetarian diet spot on. If the vegetarian eats dairy, this can also be added. Pescetarians can add in a little fish and seafood. Red meat is not a priority on this diet, in fact, it is discouraged as a regular food choice. It is listed as a once in a while food or something that can be eaten monthly, not weekly or daily. Vegetarians will find heaps of options, combinations, and recipes that meet their needs without getting the common sense of having to modify overly. This diet is a great fit and can be a foundation for a healthy vegetarian diet overall.

Keep these mistakes and misconceptions in mind and trust that this will come naturally in no time. You'll be telling your friends how good you feel and how easy it is to feed your family. You'll be giving hints on how to eat well on a budget too. Don't fall into any traps, keep it light and stick with it.

Conclusion

The best diet is one that makes you healthy and keeps you healthy, but it does not have to be boring or full of colorless, tasteless foods. Moderation is the key for any new diet to work properly. Letting go of foods rich in fats, salt and sugar might seem like a sacrifice at first. Leaving these things behind can seem tough for a moment. When you set your sights on all of the possibilities within the realm of the Mediterranean Diet, you won't be missing these things for long. You will discover just how much sweetness and flavor come straight from the earth. Adding sugar or reaching out for processed foods will soon be a distant memory and you may even wonder how you stuck with those habits for so long. Don't worry about it. The time is now and you are doing yourself a favor.

And don't worry about being bored! The Mediterranean Diet is anything but boring. The range of colors in the fresh fruits and vegetables can quickly cure you of that. Your palette will awaken to the miraculous tastes of herbs, spices and lots of natural flavors. Replacing white rice with quinoa would be a welcomed change. It will be easy to notice how the new tastes and textures enrich your eating experience. Use this diet as an excuse to be creative. Explore new foods and recipes. Learn how to cook in new ways. Invite friends over to experience your love for food and show off your new skills.

Your body deserves to be treated great. You deserve an energized body, a clear-thinking brain and a rich social life. The quality of food and the active lifestyle will take care of your body. The absence of large quantities of sugar as well as getting rid of artificial and processed foods from your diet will significantly help your mind. You will probably sleep better as well. The social aspect of this lifestyle – breaking bread (or veggies) together – will deepen the bonds of your relationships as well as your sense of being connected to your family and friends. This is a lifestyle change. It will provide you benefits immediately and into the future. This is a lifestyle that is designed to be maintained.

Eat and be merry. Enjoy cooking while sipping a glass of wine. Be good to your body and the rest will follow.

Finally, we would like to ask you to give a short, honest, and unbiased review of this book.

Please & Thank you!

Click HERE to Leave a Review for this Book!

Instant Access to Free Book Package!

As a thank you for the purchase of this book, I want to offer you some more material. We collaborate with multiple other authors specializing in various fields. We have best-selling, master writers in history, biographies, DIY projects, home improvement, arts & crafts and much more! We make a promise to you to deliver at least 4 books a week in different genres, a value of $20-30, for FREE!

All you need to do is sign up your email here at http://nextstopsuccess.net/freebooks to join our Book Club. You will get a weekly notification for more free books, courtesy of the First Class Book Club.

As a special thank you, we don't want you to wait until next week for these 4 free books. We want to give you 4 **RIGHT NOW**.

Here's what you will be getting:

- A fitness book called "BOSU Workout Routine Made Easy!"

- A book on Jim Rohn, a master life coach: "The Best of Jim Rohn: Lessons for Life Changing Success"

- A detailed biography on Conan O'Brien, a favorite late night TV show host.

- A World War 2 Best Selling box set (2 books in 1!): "The Third Reich: Nazi Rise & Fall + World War 2: The Untold Secrets of Nazi Germany".

To get instant access to this free ebook package (a value of $25), and weekly free material, all you need to do is click the link below:

http://nextstopsuccess.net/freebooks/

Add us on Facebook: First Class Book Club

Made in the USA
Columbia, SC
11 January 2018